The Spiritual Exercises with Teilhard de Chardin

The Spiritual Exercises with Teilhard de Chardin

AUGUSTÍN UDÍAS, SJ

Paulist Press
New York / Mahwah, NJ

Photos:
Page viii: Courtesy of the French Section of the Association of Friends of Pierre Teilhard de Chardin. Used with permission.
Page 36: Courtesy of the Mémorial de Verdun, Musée de la Bataille. Used with permission.
Pages 65 and 68: Courtesy of Georgetown University archives. Used with permission.

Cover image by Luminas_Art / Pixabay.com
Cover design by Joe Gallagher
Book design by Lynn Else

Original title: *Los Ejercicios Espirituales con Teilhard de Chardin* by Agustín Udías Vallina.

Copyright © Ediciones Mensajero 2022 - Grupo de Comunicación Loyola, S. L. U. - Bilbao (Spain) gcloyola.com.

This English edition translation by Natalia Muszyńska. Copyright © Paulist Press 2024.
Text of the Spiritual Exercises of Saint Ignatius Loyola translated by Louis J. Puhl, SJ. In the public domain and used with permission.

Library of Congress Cataloging-in-Publication Data
Names: Teilhard de Chardin, Pierre, author. | Udías Vallina, Agustín, editor.
Title: The spiritual exercises with Teilhard de Chardin / [edited by] Augustín Udías Vallina, SJ.
Other titles: Mes exercises. Selections. English
Description: New York : Paulist Press, [2024] | Translation of work originally in French called Mes exercises by Teilhard de Chardin, previously published in Spanish under the title Los ejercicios espirituales con Teilhard de Chardin. | Includes bibliographical references and index. | Summary: This book presents a series of texts, taken from among the works of Teilhard that illuminate the meditations of the Exercises throughout four weeks, drawing from his vision of God, Christ, and the world. A brief introduction before each text serves to relate it to the content of each of the meditations with references to the text of Saint Ignatius"—Provided by publisher.
Identifiers: LCCN 2023016466 (print) | LCCN 2023016467 (ebook) | ISBN 9780809156719 (paperback) | ISBN 9780809188338 (e-book)
Subjects: LCSH: Spiritual exercises. | Meditations.
Classification: LCC BX2178 .T4313 2024 (print) | LCC BX2178 (ebook) | DDC 242—dc23/eng/20230802
LC record available at https://lccn.loc.gov/2023016466
LC ebook record available at https://lccn.loc.gov/2023016467

ISBN 978-0-8091-5671-9 (paperback)
ISBN 978-0-8091-8833-8 (e-book)

Published by Paulist Press
997 Macarthur Boulevard
Mahwah, New Jersey 07430
www.paulistpress.com

Printed and bound in the
United States of America

Teilhard de Chardin, New York, 1955.

CONTENTS

Contents

Contents

Teilhard and his family on a day close to his ordination, Hastings, 1911.
From left to right: Pierre, Gonzague, Joseph, their father, Victor, their mother.

LIST OF ILLUSTRATIONS

PROLOGUE

For Pierre Teilhard de Chardin, since his formation as a Jesuit and throughout his life and scientific work, the practice of the *Spiritual Exercises of Saint Ignatius* represented the core of his spiritual life. Very early, however, he felt the need to integrate into his spirituality a new vision of an evolutionary universe presented by the modern sciences, which he came across in his scientific education, a fact that could not but also influence his vision of the *Exercises*. From his first writings during the First World War, which he took part in as a stretcher-bearer, to the final ones—the very year of his death—one can find a continuous reflection of the ideas contained in the *Exercises*, although approached from new perspectives, according to his vision of the world through science and the presence of Christ in it. This book presents a series of texts, taken from among the works of Teilhard that illuminate the meditations of the *Exercises* throughout four weeks, drawing from his vision of God, Christ, and the world. A brief introduction before each text serves to relate it to the content of each of the meditations with references to the text of Saint Ignatius.

The texts of Teilhard convey a new vision of the *Exercises*, focused on the presence of Christ in an evolutionary universe that progresses, through human work, toward its final union with him. In this way, they present a new approach to the *Exercises*, centered on the presence of Christ in the world that leads us, as Teilhard states, to a vision of the "universalized Christ" and a "Christified universe." These texts reveal a new perspective of the *Exercises*, specially adapted to our times, influenced to an enormous degree by the progress of science and technology in a globalized world. The Ignatian Christocentric spirituality present in the *Exercises* receives, therefore, a new life. The quotations of the texts come from the original works in French, and in most cases, their original English translations have been used. Only a few texts have been newly translated from Spanish.

INTRODUCTION
Scientist, Philosopher, and Mystic

Pierre Teilhard de Chardin (1881–1955) was born in Sarcenat, near Orcine in Auvergne, a short distance west of Clermont-Ferrand, into a family of the French rural aristocracy.[1] He studied at the Jesuit School of Notre Dame de Mongré and in 1899 joined the novitiate of the Society of Jesus in Aix-en-Provence. Teilhard continued his studies of humanities and philosophy on the English island of Jersey, where the French Jesuits had settled due to emergency laws of 1901 in France. During these studies, Teilhard became interested in geology. Between 1905 and 1908, he was a professor of physics and chemistry at the Jesuit School of the Holy Family in Cairo. It was his first contact with the East that would fascinate him later and the place where he continued his passion for geology and carried out his first field work, searching for fossils. He completed his theological studies in Hastings (Sussex, England), where he was ordained a priest in August 1911 and where his interest in geology and paleontology was further developed. It was also here where he met Charles Dawson and was involved in the discovery of the "man from Piltdown," which turned out to be a forgery. Later, when Teilhard was already famous, some wanted to hold him unjustly responsible for the deception.

The Spiritual Exercises with Teilhard de Chardin

From 1912 to 1914, Teilhard studied geology and paleontology in Paris under the direction of Marcellin Boule, the head of the Institute of Human Paleontology of the National Museum of Natural History, known in French as the *Muséum national d'histoire naturelle* (MNHN) and also a native of Auvergne. He introduced Teilhard to paleontological studies. With Henri Breuil, an ecclesiastic and a paleontologist, whom he also met then, Teilhard would maintain a close relationship throughout his life. In those years, he carried out several study trips together with a group of scientists, including trips to the caves with prehistoric remains and paintings in southern France and northern Spain (Altamira and Puente Viesgo, Cantabria) and to the Alps, Normandy, and England. In 1915, Teilhard was mobilized as a stretcher-bearer in a mixed regiment of French and North Africans, and until 1919, he lived the experience of the war, which marked him deeply and which he interpreted as a "baptism into the real," that is, immersion into the large human confrontation that the First World War represented. During that time, Teilhard said to Fr. Victor Fontoynont, "These thirty months have been like a long spiritual retreat. I have become at the same time very mystical and very realistic."[2] While Teilhard was at the front, he wrote the first (nineteen) essays outlining his philosophical and theological thinking, which he sent to his cousin, Marguerite Teillard-Chambon.[3] Many of the ideas and a considerable part of the spirituality that he developed later are contained in them. His commitment and courage in caring for the wounded at the front earned him the War Cross (1915), the Military Medal (1917), and the Legion of Honor (1920). After the war, he returned to Paris, where he completed his degree in natural sciences in 1919 and began teaching geology at the Catholic University of Paris (Institut Catholique de Paris), soon to be interrupted. The following year, he presented his doctoral thesis on the early Eocene mammals in France, for which he was awarded the prize of the Geological Society of France. Teilhard continued working at the Museum and at the Institute of Human Paleontology and was a professor of geology at the Institut Catholique.

In 1923, invited by the Jesuit Émile Licent (1876–1952), who was forming a museum of natural history in Tianjin, Teilhard made his first trip to China, where he worked on the geology of northern China and Mongolia. In particular, he accompanied Licent in a long geological field study in the Ordos Desert. In 1924, upon his return to Paris, Teilhard encountered his first problem with the ecclesiastical authorities, following an essay on original sin that had arrived in Rome without his knowledge. This resulted in his resignation as a professor at the Institut Catholique and a second trip to China, as his presence in Paris was becoming uncomfortable. As a result of these trips, his life became linked to geological and paleontological work in China, where, starting in 1929, he collaborated with the National Geological Survey of China. His time was shared between China and France, where he continued working at the Museum. In 1926, he began working at the Choukoutien fossil deposit, with the human fossils of *Sinanthropus* (*Homo erectus pekinensis*). The study of human fossils became his most important line of research. In Tientsin, between November 1926 and March 1927, he wrote *The Divine Milieu* (*Le Milieu divin*), the most complete work on his vision of Christian spirituality.

In 1931, he participated as a geologist in the Yellow Cruise, a nine-month trip from Beijing to Turkestan through Central Asia, organized by the Citroën factory as a demonstration of its cars. Between 1932 and 1937, he worked at Peking Man Museum, with frequent trips to France. In 1935, he carried out geological work in northern India in the company of geologists George Barbour, Davidson Black, and Helmut de Terra, with whom he maintained a close friendship. And in 1938, he traveled to Java at the invitation of Gustav von Koenigswald, who discovered human fossils in that region. By 1939, Teilhard was already a recognized figure in the scientific circles of human paleontology; he traveled, offered lectures in France and the United States, and carried out fieldwork in collaboration with other scientists. In addition to those already mentioned in China, Kashmir, and Java, his studies also expanded to Burma and South Africa, linking his work increasingly to the research of human origins. In 1947, he was appointed an officer of the Legion of Honor and a corresponding member of the Académie des Sciences.

His ideas on evolution and its impact on the formulation of the Christian faith were beginning to be widely discussed in France. At a time when the theory of evolution was still viewed with reservations in ecclesiastical circles, Teilhard's ideas met with increasing suspicion and rejection. He was not allowed to publish, except for purely scientific works, although copies of his essays were disseminated widely among his many enthusiastic followers. His presence in France had been uncomfortable for years, and he stayed away as long as possible. Between June 1947 and 1948, he wrote the definitive work presenting his thinking, *The Human Phenomenon* (*Le phénomène humain*). In October 1948, Teilhard traveled to Rome to seek permission to publish this work that he failed to obtain and, at the same time, was denied permission to enter the prestigious Collège de France. Despite everything, his loyalty to the Church and to the Society remained unshakable.

From 1952 onward, his stays in New York became longer. There, at the Wenner-Gren Foundation, he carried on with his work on human paleontology and wrote two important essays: *The Heart of Matter* (1950) and *The Christic* (1955). On Easter Sunday, 1955, he died in New York.

TEILHARD'S VISION OF THE *SPIRITUAL EXERCISES*

As a Jesuit priest and at the same time a renowned scientist in the fields of geology and paleontology, Teilhard de Chardin's greatest concern was always how to integrate Christian thought and Ignatian spirituality into the new worldview proposed by the sciences of an evolving world in an immense space-time. This integration is shown in his numerous nonscientific writings.[4] In particular, for Teilhard, as for every Jesuit, the *Spiritual Exercises of Saint Ignatius of Loyola* represented a central point of his life and spirituality. After his formation as a Jesuit, during which he carried out a full thirty-day retreat of the *Exercises*—twice in the novitiate and the third during his tertianship—he faithfully did the eight-day annual retreat of the *Exercises* many times during his long boat trips. Fortunately, we have his notes of the *Exercises* from 1919 to 1954, missing only those from the years 1933 to 1938.[5] These notes, written for himself, show us the most intimate part of the evolution of his spirituality throughout his life, and his conception and practice of the *Exercises*. We do not know if Teilhard directed the *Exercises* for others in the traditional sense, but there is no doubt that the fundamental ideas of the *Exercises* were present in his retreats, talks, lectures, conversations, and writings.

Special characteristics of Teilhard's spirituality, marked by the scientific vision of an evolving world, are also reflected in his conception and practice of the *Exercises*.[6] In a work written a month before his death, he claims that young Jesuits dedicated to science should be educated to discern and find the "Christic" element in and through the "Ultrahuman" element in their religious formation. Teilhard understands the *Christic* as the presence of Christ in the world through his incarnation, and the *Ultrahuman* as the last stage of human evolution. For him, cosmic evolution is thus completed by the union in the "Omega Christ," the goal of the whole evolution. In this way, the spiritual formation of Jesuit students, Teilhard says,

> would take the form of the practice of the *Exercises*, rethought (exactly as in the case of dogma) along the lines of a clearer appreciation of the virtues, at once Christic and Christifying, to be found in man's works

and activities. "The Foundation," "The Kingdom," "The Two Standards"…since those essential meditations were conceived at a time when man was still regarded as inserted, fully formed, in a static universe […] They do not accord to the progress of hominization its full value of sanctifying and of producing communion.[7]

Teilhard was very clear, therefore, that the meditations of the *Exercises* had to be adapted to the new evolutionary vision of the universe and of man that science provides today. The essential meditations of the *Exercises*—Principle and Foundation, The Kingdom, The Two Standards, and so on—conceived from the point of view of a static universe, should be adapted to the vision of a dynamic, evolving one, which continues, through human work, attracted by the activity of the "Total Christ," toward whom the whole universe tends.

This adaptation of the *Exercises* can be found explicitly formulated in Teilhard's notes of the *Exercises* of the year 1952.[8] He begins by referring to the *Exercises* as "no longer 'the' Exercises; but (very humbly…and because I am inwardly *forced*) MY *Exercises* [*MES Exercises*]." His capitalization of "my" emphasizes the personal and proper aspect of his vision and practice of the *Exercises* that he also calls "the Trans-Exercises" (*les Trans-Exercices*). That is, as if they were actually beyond the traditional formulation. In this way, the meditations on the Foundation, Sin, Christ, the Cross take on a new dimension and a kind of "new heart." He now calls them, putting before them the *neo-* prefix: the New Foundation, the New Sin, the New Christ, the New Cross (*le néo-Fondement, le Néo-péché, le néo-Christ, la néo-Croix*). The four weeks of the *Exercises* also take on new names, in which the *neo*-prefix appears as well: the 1st, Neo-Creation (Divine Milieu and God-Omega); the 2nd, Neo-Incarnation; the 3rd, Neo-Redemption; the 4th, Neo-Pleromization. By *pleromization* Teilhard means the final realization or pleroma (fullness) of the universe and humanity in Omega

Christ, in which, according to Paul, Christ will be all in all (Col 3:11). We can see that the four weeks are in fact kept according to the Ignatian scheme but are reformulated according to Teilhard's vision of the world and the role of Christ in it. In the rest of the notes from that year, we find a development of this new concept of the *Exercises*. In a letter from the same year, 1952, to his friend Fr. Pierre Leroy, with whom he shared several years in China, Teilhard writes about the *Exercises* he is going to do in accordance with this new vision which, as he says, "he is sure that Fr. Ignatius will approve." However, he recognizes that he has to affirm, "more deeply than ever [...] the gulf that has been created little by little between his religious vision of the World and the one of the Exercises....A 'gulf' not of contradiction, but of expansion."[9] He clarifies thus that the fundamentals of the *Exercises* are maintained, but they are now seen from a new perspective that opens up to new visions of the world and the presence of Christ in it.

In his notes, we find other texts in which Teilhard shows how the *Exercises* should be modified to adapt to modern times.[10] For example, in the *Exercises* of 1940, he writes, "Nothing in common between my attitude and that of Saint Ignatius. In such times, he seeks conversion by a sort of 'fundamentalism,' while I favor 'integralism' (over-humanism)."[11] Later, in the *Exercises* themselves, looking to the future and the new ways of performing the *Exercises* that he proposed, he writes, "Who will be the new Saint Ignatius and his blessed companions? They may, after all, come out of my dust!"[12] We see, therefore, how Teilhard conceives the practice of the *Exercises* in a new way, within his evolutionary vision of the world and the central role of Christ in it.

These ideas about the new approaches to the *Exercises*, in accordance with Teilhard's own Christian vision that he himself summarizes as "a religion of 'Christianzed' evolution or an *evolved* Christianity,"[13] must be taken into account when considering the texts that we propose within the framework of the *Exercises* throughout the four weeks. The texts reveal a new vision of the traditional meditations of the *Exercises* and the most central aspects of Ignatian spirituality. For those unfamiliar with Teilhard's ideas and particularly his Christology, some things may seem strange. Let us be impressed, however, by these texts, which show us a new vision of *The Spiritual Exercises of Saint Ignatius*, the fruit of a profound mystical experience of Christ's presence in the world formulated in a new way. A different approach to the *Exercises* according to the spirit of Teilhard is the one that can be found in the work of Louis Savary, in which the meditations are tackled according to the Teilhardian viewpoint, but Teilhard's texts are not provided for them.[14]

FIRST WEEK

PRINCIPLE AND FOUNDATION

Saint Ignatius begins the experience of the *Spiritual Exercises* with an introductory consideration that he titles "Principle and Foundation" and in which he places man before the creator and reminds him of the reason for his existence, the thing for which he has been created, that is, "to praise, reverence and serve God his Lord." Immediately, he adds the place and role of other things: "And the other things on the face of the earth are created for man that they may help him in prosecuting the end for which he is created."[1] Therefore, we have here a proposed relationship between man and the world. Following the outlook of his time, the world for Saint Ignatius is the external and static environment in which man is situated and that has been created by God to help him. For Teilhard, this is the evolving world presented by the modern sciences, of which man is an integral part and contributes to its evolution.

However, while Saint Ignatius in the *Exercises* does not raise the problem of faith but rather takes it for granted, Teilhard, aware of the modern secularized world in which we live, does raise it in the first place and establishes, as he says, "the true Foundation": "For me, that is the true Foundation. To really believe that you exist, my God….The whole difficulty is there, I think, for everyone. If one is 'indifferent,' this is what they dare not risk, on the uncertain, the inconsistent....Oh, who will make us, God, *real*, *consistent*! Is this really possible...." He finishes, demanding, "In order that I may feel not only your presence, but also your Existence, make me recognize it, but above all, reveal yourself to me, Jesus."[2] In our consideration of the Principle and Foundation, let us also begin by acknowledging our lack of faith and the need for God to increase it for us.

AN EVOLVING WORLD

For Teilhard, humanity, on the one hand, is part of the universe and, thus, is not something external to it. On the other hand, his vision of the universe is the evolutionary universe discovered by science, and humanity is also part of that evolution, both biological and cosmic. It is, therefore, a dynamic, not static, vision of the evolving universe, and humankind is not simply "placed" in it but is part of it and its evolution and contributes with their works. Humanity's relationship with it is not simply to "use other things" but, as a part of them, to bring the whole universe to its culmination in the convergence in God, the "Omega Point," by an evolutionary process of unification, which is also the way in which God has created the world. We can thus begin with his vision of the universe and humanity, from the point of view of what he calls the "Creative Union," which is, for him, the active process of evolution, and consider in this way the role of humanity, the relationship between matter and spirit, and the unifying process that governs all evolution. But without forgetting the divine breath present in creation: "What is divine, in the World, is LIFE and what is NECESSARY—and *matter*. *Life*, which is the creative *aspiration*; Matter, which is *union* and *integration*, final incorporation into order, cosmic energy, subjection to forces and monads."[3] Let us begin, in this way, accompanied by Teilhard, with the Principle and Foundation, and with the vision of the creative union through which God becomes present and acts in the world.

The creative Union is not exactly a metaphysical doctrine. It is rather a sort of empirical and pragmatic explanation of the universe, conceived in my mind from the need to reconcile in a solidly coherent system scientific views on evolution (accepted as, in their essence, definitively established) with the innate urge that has impelled me to look for the Divine not in a cleavage with the physical world but through matter, and, in some sort of way, in union with matter....

The creative Union is the theory that accepts this proposition: in the present evolutionary phase of the cosmos (the only phase known to us), everything happens as though the One were formed by successive unifications of the Multiple. [...] At the lower limit of things, too deep for any of us to penetrate, it discloses an immense plurality—complete diversity combined with total disunity. This absolute multiplicity would, in truth, be nothingness, and it has never existed. But it is the quarter from which the world emerges for us: at the beginning of all time, the world appears to us rising up from the Multiple, impregnated with and still bedewed with the Multiple. Already, however, since something exists, the work of unification has begun. [...] Only in man, so far as we know, does spirit so perfectly unite around itself the universality of the universe that, despite the momentary dissociation of its organic foundation, nothing can any longer destroy the "vortex" of operation and consciousness of which it is the subsisting centre. The human soul is the first fully formed purchase point that the Multiple can fasten onto as it is drawn up by the Creation towards unity....

Matter and Spirit are not opposed as two separate things, as two natures, but as two directions of evolution within the world. [...] On any hypothesis, if the world is to be thinkable it must be centred. The presence, therefore, at its head, of an Omega [...] that the position of universal centre has not been given to any supreme intermediary between God and the Universe, but has been occupied by the Divinity himself.[4]

A MATERIAL WORLD

Matter has sometimes been related to evil and, even today, we are left with the remnants of this understanding. As we contemplate the material universe that surrounds us and of which we are part as a link in evolution, we run the risk of keeping some attitudes still tinged with Manichaeism and an implicit dualism between matter and spirit of a neo-gnostic character. We often look with some suspicion at what has to do with the material. Teilhard distinguishes two zones in matter: one is the zone of matter understood "*in the material and carnal sense*; and the zone offered to our renewed efforts towards progress, search, conquest and 'divinisation,' the zone of matter *taken in the spiritual sense.*" It contains "a certain quantity of spiritual power."[5] In this way, Teilhard finds in matter itself a "spiritual dimension." Moreover, matter, in the end, has been divinized by the incarnation in the Body of Christ. Therefore, it is good that we also learn to contemplate the material universe and matter in us, our bodies, and see them with new eyes. Teilhard encourages us to contemplate the "blessed matter" and sing with him a hymn in its honor:

Blessed be you, harsh Matter, barren soil, stubborn rock: you who yield only to violence, you who force us to work if we would eat.

Blessed be you, perilous Matter, violent sea, untameable passion: you who unless we fetter you will devour us.

Blessed be you, mighty Matter, irresistible march of evolution, reality ever new-born; you who, by constantly shattering our mental categories, force us to go ever further and further in our pursuit of the truth.

Blessed be you, universal Matter, immeasurable time, boundless ether, triple abyss of stars and atoms and generations: you who by overflowing and dissolving our narrow standards or measurement reveal to us the dimensions of God.

Blessed be you, impenetrable Matter: you who, interposed between our minds and the world of essences, cause us to languish with the desire to pierce through the seamless veil of phenomena.

Blessed be you, mortal Matter: you who one day will undergo the process of dissolution within us and will thereby take us forcibly into the very heart of that which exists.

Without you, Matter, without your onslaughts, without your uprooting of us, we should remain all our lives inert, stagnant, puerile, ignorant both of ourselves and of God.

You who batter us and then dress our wounds, you who resist us and yield to us, you who wreck and build, you who shackle and liberate, the sap of our souls, the hand of God, the flesh of Christ: it is you, Matter, that I bless....

If we are ever to reach you, Matter, we must, having first established contact with the totality of all that lives and moves here below, come little by little to feel that the individual shapes of all we have laid hold on are melting away in our hands, until finally, we are until we are caught by *the substance* of all consistencies and all unions.

If we are ever to possess you, having taken you rapturously in our arms, we must then go on to sublimate you through sorrow.

Your realm, Matter, comprises those serene heights where saints think to avoid you—but where your flesh is so transparent and so agile as to be no longer distinguishable from spirit.

Raise me up then, Matter, to those heights, through struggle and separation and death; raise me up until, at long last, it becomes possible for me in perfect chastity to embrace the universe.[6]

HUMAN BEINGS AND THEIR WORKS

Human beings and the works of their hands are also part of the universe that Saint Ignatius offers for our consideration at this beginning of the *Exercises*. For Teilhard, the evolutionary process of the world does not end with the appearance of humankind but continues precisely through the works of humanity, particularly scientific-technical progress. The evolution of humanity, the "noosphere" (sphere of thought), as he calls it, is part of the cosmic evolution that, while it must be convergent, will end with the final union in God, the Omega Point of creation. This idea should never be missing in our consideration of the world in which we live today. Teilhard, in particular, encourages us to contemplate every human progress, especially the scientific-technical one, which today fills all aspects of human life and spreads throughout the world, and to see it, with its ups and downs, as part of the journey of humankind toward God.

Our picture is of mankind labouring under the impulsion of an obscure instinct, so as to break out through its narrow point of emergence and submerge the earth; of thought becoming numerous so as to conquer all habitable space, taking precedence over all other forms of life; of mind, in other words, deploying and convoluting the layers of the noosphere. This effort at multiplication and organic expansion is, for him who can see, the summing up and final expression of human prehistory and history, from the earliest beginnings down to the present day....

The age of industry; the age of oil, electricity and the atom; the age of the machine, of huge communities and of science—the future will decide what is the best name to describe the era we are entering. The word matters little. What does matter is that we should be told that, at the cost of what we are enduring, life is taking a step, and a decisive step, in us and in our environment....

No one would dare to picture to himself what the noosphere will be like in its final guise, no one, that is, who has glimpsed however faintly the incredible potential of unexpectedness accumulated in the spirit of the earth. The end of the world defies imagination. But if it would be absurd to try to describe it, we may none the less—by making use of the lines of approach already laid down—foresee to some extent the significance and circumscribe the forms....

The end of the world: the wholesale internal introversion upon itself of the noosphere, which has simultaneously reached the uttermost limit of its complexity and its centrality.

The end of the world: the overthrow of equilibrium, detaching the mind, fulfilled at last, from its material matrix, so that it will henceforth rest with all its weight on God-Omega.

The end of the world: critical point simultaneously of emergence and emersion, of maturation and escape.[7]

THE POWER OF LOVE

For Teilhard, the line of cosmic evolution is the increase in complexity, through the union, from the elementary particles of the *Big Bang* to atoms, molecules, and increasingly complex chemical compounds, and in living beings, from the simplest ones to humankind. On the human level, evolution progresses through the increase in socialization (the union between humanity), so that the acting uniting force is, in the end, the power of love. In some way, through all the forms of attraction present in the world, we can already see manifestations of the force of a kind of generalized love. Thus, for Teilhard, love is the strongest cosmic power, a power of unification and spiritualization present at all levels of the universe, in particular at the human level. He recognizes in it a reflection of God's own attraction for everything that has been created.

> Love is the most universal, the most tremendous and the most mysterious of the cosmic forces. After centuries of tentative effort, social institutions have externally sought to save and channel it....
>
> Is it truly possible for humanity to continue to live and grow without asking itself how much truth and energy it is losing by neglecting its incredible power of love?
>
> From the standpoint of spiritual evolution, which we here assume, it seems that we can give a name and value to this strange energy of love. Can we not say quite simply that in its essence it is the attraction exercised on each unit of consciousness by the centre of the

universe in the course of taking shape? It calls us to the great union, the realization of which is the only process at present taking place in nature.

By this hypothesis, according to which (in agreement with the findings of psychological analysis) love is the primal and universal psychic energy, does not everything become clear around us, both for our minds and our actions? [...]

The most telling and profound way of describing the evolution of the universe would undoubtedly be to trace the evolution of love.[8]

LOVE AND THE FEMININE

On a human level, we find the feminine as a symbol of love. Teilhard expresses his celebration in his poetic writing "The Eternal Feminine." Considering the relationship between humanity and the surrounding universe and of human beings among themselves—which is what Saint Ignatius wants the retreatant to begin their experience of the *Exercises* with—we cannot leave out the consideration of the power of love that is making us progress united toward God and that we find symbolized in the feminine, the union of man and woman. As we have seen, we find this force acting in the universe at all levels, from its beginning in the attractions of elementary particles, in living beings, and especially in men and women. Teilhard sees in the feminine a symbol of this cosmic energy of love. That's how he starts personifying the feminine.

When the world was born, I came into being. Before the centuries were made, I issued from the hand of God—half-formed, yet destined to grow in beauty from age to age, the handmaid of his work. Everything in the universe is made by union and generation—by the coming together of elements that seek out one another, melt together two by two, and are born again in a third.

God instilled me into the initial multiple as a force of condensation and concentration.

In me is seen that side of beings by which they are joined as one, in me the fragrance that makes them hasten together and leads them, freely and passionately, along their road to unity.

Through me, all things have their movement and are made to work as one.

I am the beauty running through the world, to make it associate in ordered groups: the ideal held up before the world to make it ascend.

I am the essential Feminine....

Faced by a mankind that never ceases to ascend, the part I have to play insists on my withdrawing to an ever-higher level—held aloft, over the earth's growing ambition, as a lure and a prize—almost grasped, but never held. By its very nature, the Feminine must continue unremittingly to make itself progressively more felt in a universe that has not reached the term of its evolution: to ensure the final blossoming of my stock, will be the glory and bliss of chastity. Countless are the new essences handed over by nature, from age to age, to life!

Under the influence of Christianity, I shall combine, until creation is complete, their subtle and dangerous refinements in an ever-changing perfection which will embrace the aspirations of each new generation....

And at that moment you may see with wonder how there unfolds, in the long web of my charms, the ever-living series of allurements—of forces that one after another have made themselves felt ever since the borderline of nothingness, and so brought together and assembled the elements of Spirit—through love. I am the Eternal Feminine.[9]

THE CONVERGENCE OF THE WORLD IN GOD

Teilhard emphasizes that the evolution of the universe, including the action of human beings in the progress of humanity, must eventually be convergent, have an end in a definitive unity. Teilhard sees humanity or the noosphere as driven by the force of love toward a growing unification. However, the elements of the noosphere, that is, the individual persons, are free to choose their future. How do these two things fit together—the freedom and the union implicated in the Spirit of the Earth? To ensure convergence toward unity, Teilhard has to propose the existence of a new and definitive attraction that controls the movements of the elements of the noosphere. Its influence, in order to preserve freedom, resembles that of "seduction" and is caused by a super-personal center, the Omega Point, which religions call God, who acts from and on freedom.

As in the plane of the noosphere the unifying movement is driven by the power of love, the Omega Point can only have influence through a true "super-love." The unifying convergence of the noosphere is thus assured and will reach its fulfillment in the final focal point of the cosmic evolution. For the Christian, the divine Omega Point is identified with Christ, God incarnate in the world, and it is precisely thanks to his presence and attraction by love that the final convergence in him takes place. With this text, we want to conclude the consideration of the universe and humanity in it, requested by the Principle and Foundation, a universe not only as created by God but ultimately oriented and attracted to him and by him, through the activity of human beings.

It is therefore a mistake to look for the extension of our being or of the noosphere in the Impersonal. The Future-Universal could not be anything else but the Hyper-Personal—at the Omega Point. […] For the failure that threatens us to be turned into success, for the concurrence of human monads to come about, it is necessary and sufficient for us that we should extend our science to its farthest limits and recognise and accept (as being necessary to close and balance space-time) not only some vague future existence, but also, as I must now stress, the radiation *as a present reality* of that mysterious centre of our centres which I have called Omega. […] Expressed in terms of internal energy, the cosmic function of Omega consists in initiating and maintaining within its radius the unanimity of the world's "reflective" particles.

In Omega we have in the first place the principle we needed to explain both the persistent march of things towards greater consciousness, and the paradoxical solidity of what is most fragile. […] All around us, one by one, like a continual exhalation, "souls" break away, carrying upwards their incommunicable load of consciousness. One by one, yet not in isolation. Since, for each of them, by the very nature of Omega, there can only be one possible point of definitive emersion—that point at which, under the synthesising action of personalising union, the noosphere (furling its elements upon themselves as it too furls upon itself) will reach collectively its point of convergence—at the "end of the world."[10]

OUR ACTIVITIES

After the introductory consideration of the Principle and Foundation for the first week of the *Exercises*, Saint Ignatius suggests a meditation on sins: "The first exercise is a meditation on the three powers on the first, the second and the third sin."[11] Previously, he has proposed the practice of examination, the "particular and everyday" one, as well as the "general" one and the "general confession." It is in the spirit of these considerations that Teilhard's texts on the activities and passivities of our lives are offered.

We have seen the tremendous extent and complexity of the God-created universe around us, of whose evolution we are part, and the work of human beings to drive progress as part of that evolution. The first question we can ask ourselves is what our role is in it and, thus, we turn our gaze to our activities. Sometimes we run the risk of seeing the value of our activities only from the spiritual viewpoint, focusing only on pious or charitable actions. We think that the rest of them only have value in the intention for which we do them and not in themselves. For Teilhard, this is a mistake, since all actions have a value in themselves whenever they collaborate in the construction of the world, which is the work that God has entrusted to human beings. They form, indeed, the continuation of cosmic evolution on the human level. So, as he says, "we should be passionate about the things of the Earth."

> The great objection brought against Christianity in our time, and the real source of the distrust which insulates entire blocks of humanity from the influence of the Church, has nothing to do with historical or theological difficulties. It is the suspicion that our religion makes its followers inhuman. "Christianity," so some of the best of the Gentiles are inclined to think, "is bad or inferior" because it does not lead its followers to levels of attainment beyond ordinary human powers; rather it withdraws them from the ordinary ways of humankind and sets them on other paths....
>
> But do not blame anything but our weakness: our faith imposes on us the right and the duty to throw

ourselves into the things of the earth. As much as you, and even better than you (because, of the two of us, I alone am in a position to prolong the perspectives of my endeavour to infinity, in conformity with the requirements of my present intention), I want to dedicate myself body and soul to the sacred duty of research. We must test every barrier, try every path, plumb every abyss. *Nihil intentatum* [Nothing untried]....God wills it, who willed that he should have need of it. You are men, you say? *Plus et ego* [I am more].

There can be no doubt of it. At a time when the consciousness of its own powers and possibilities is legitimately awakening in a humanity now ready to become adult, one of the first duties of a Christian as an apologist is to show, by the logic of his religious views and still more by the logic of his action, that the incarnate God did not come to diminish in us the glorious responsibility and splendid ambition that is ours: of fashioning our own self. Once again, *non minuit, sed sacravit* [not diminished, but consecrated]. No, Christianity is not, as it is sometimes presented and sometimes practised, an additional burden of observances and obligations to weigh down and increase the already heavy load, or to multiply the already paralysing ties of our life in society. It is, in fact, a soul of immense power which bestows significance and beauty and a new lightness on what we are already doing. It is true that it sets us on the road towards unsuspected heights. But the slope which leads to these heights is linked so closely with the one we were already climbing naturally, that there is nothing so distinctively human in the Christian (and this is what remains to be considered) as his detachment.[12]

THE DIVINIZATION OF ACTIVITIES

Responding to the vision of our effort and activities in the context of world progress, Teilhard believes in their divinization. For this purpose, our acts must be instruments in the creative work of God, and Christ must be present in them through his incarnation. Moreover, our actions are not only instruments of God's creative work, but their living extension. In this way, we ask that our activities and works themselves be kept by God in eternity, for they are part of ourselves. Teilhard believes that, in some mysterious way, our works too will be preserved in eternal life as part of the new earth and the promised new heavens.

Each one of our works, by its more or less remote or direct effect upon the spiritual world, helps to make perfect Christ in his mystical totality. That is the fullest possible answer to the question: How can we, following the call of St. Paul, see God in all the active half of our lives? In fact, through the unceasing operation of the Incarnation, the divine so thoroughly permeates all our creaturely energies that, in order to meet it and lay hold on it, we could not find a more fitting setting than that of our action.

To begin with, in action I adhere to the creative power of God; I coincide with it; I become not only its instrument but its living extension. And as there is nothing more personal in a being than his will, I merge myself, in a sense, through my heart, with the very heart of God. This contact is continuous because I am always acting; and at the same time, since I can never set a boundary to the perfection of my fidelity nor to the fervour of my intention, it enables me to liken myself, ever more strictly and indefinitely, to God.

The soul does not pause to relish this communion, nor does it lose sight of the material end of its action; for it is wedded to a *creative* effort. The will to succeed, a certain passionate delight in the work to be done, form an integral part of our creaturely fidelity. It follows that the very sincerity with which we desire and pursue success for God's sake reveals itself as a new factor—also without limits—in our being knit together with him who animates us. [...] Indeed, without exaggeration or excess in thought or expression—but simply by confronting the most fundamental truths of our faith and of experience—we are led to the following observation: God is inexhaustibly attainable in the *totality* of our action. And this outstanding example of divinisation has nothing with which we dare to compare it except the subtle, gentle sweetness with which this actual change of shape is wrought; for it is achieved without disturbing in any way (*non minuit, sed sacravit* [not diminished, but consecrated]...) the perfection and unity of human effort.

But will not the work itself of our minds, of our hearts, and of our hands—that is to say, our achievements, what we bring into being, our *opus* [work]—will not this, too, in some sense be "eternalised" and saved? Indeed, Lord, it will be—by virtue of a claim which you yourself have implanted at the very centre of my will! I desire and need that it should be....

I desire it because I love irresistibly all that your continuous help enables me to bring each day to reality. A thought, a material improvement, a harmony, a unique nuance of human Love, the enchanting complexity of a smile or a glance, all these new beauties that appear for the first time, in me or around me, on the human face of the earth—I cherish them like children and cannot believe that they will die entirely in their flesh. I believed that these things were to perish for ever, should I have given them life? The more I examine myself, the more I discover this psychological truth: that no one lifts his little finger to do the smallest task unless moved, however obscurely, by the conviction that he is contributing infinitesimally (at least indirectly) to the building of something definitive—that is to say, to your work, my God.[13]

THE DIVINIZATION OF THE WORLD

Through the divinization of our activities, the phenomenon of divinization of the world itself takes place. Teilhard goes one step further and affirms that this divinization is done in Christ: "A Christian can be recognized by his role of divinizing the world in Jesus Christ." In this way, the activities marked with human effort acquire a new meaning, above all individual and collective interests. We are building the whole world through our effort, but that world is a world created by God. He has become incarnate in Christ in the world, which is destined to be fulfilled in him. For this reason, Teilhard can repeat again and again: "By virtue of the Creation and, still more, of the Incarnation, *nothing here below is profane* for those who know how to see. On the contrary, everything is *sacred* to the men who can distinguish that portion of chosen being which is subject to Christ's drawing power in the process of consummation."[14]

It is in the Christian, provided he knows how to make the most of the resources of his faith, that these effects will reach their climax and their crown. As we have seen: from the point of view of the reality, accuracy and splendour of the ultimate end towards which we must aim in the least of our acts, we, disciples of Christ, are the most favoured of men. The Christian knows that his function is to divinise the world in Jesus Christ. In him, therefore, the natural process which drives human action from ideal to ideal and towards objects ever more internally coherent and comprehensive in their embrace, reaches—thanks to the support of Revelation—its fullest expansion. And in him, consequently, detachment through action should produce its maximum effectiveness.

And this is perfectly true. The Christian as we have described him in these pages, is at once the most attached and the most detached of men. Convinced in a way in which the "worldly" cannot be of the unfathomable importance and value concealed beneath the humblest worldly success, the Christian is at the same time as convinced as the hermit of the worthlessness of any success which is envisaged only as a benefit to himself (or even a general one) without reference to God. It is God and God alone whom he pursues through the reality of created things. For him, interest lies truly in things, but in absolute dependence upon God's presence in them. The light of heaven becomes perceptible and attainable to him in the crystalline transparency of beings. But he wants only this light, and if the light is extinguished, whether because the object is out of its true place, or has outlived its function, or has moved itself, then even the most precious substance is only ashes in his sight. Similarly, within himself and his most personal development, it is not himself that he is seeking, but that which is greater than he, to which he knows that he is destined. In his own view he himself no longer counts, no longer exists; he has forgotten and lost himself in the very endeavour which is making him perfect. It is no longer the atom which lives, but the universe within it.

Not only has he encountered God in the entire field of his actions in the perceptible world, but in the course of this first phase of his spiritual development, the divine milieu which has been uncovered absorbs his powers in the very proportion in which these laboriously rise above their individuality.[...]

Show all your faithful, Lord, in what a full and true sense "their work follows them" into your kingdom— *opera sequuntur illos.* Otherwise they will become like those idle workmen who are not spurred by their task. And even if a sound human instinct prevails over their hesitancies or the sophisms of an incompletely enlightened religious practice, they will remain fundamentally divided and frustrated; and it will be said that the sons of heaven cannot compete on the human level, in conviction and hence on equal terms, with the children of the world.[15]

PASSIVITIES OF DIMINISHMENT

For Teilhard, the other aspect of our lives, in addition to activities, is the negative, which he groups under the term "passivities of diminishment." They include everything that happens to us of a somehow negative character: for example, adversities, sufferings, aging, diseases, and finally our death. With passivities, he distinguishes between those of internal origin and those of external origin, those born within ourselves and those that come from outside. The added term of *diminishment* makes us recognize that we experience them as something diminishing us. But Teilhard emphasizes that, just as in activities, we are the one who acts, in passivities, it is God who acts in us. Despite the difficulty in acknowledging it, the hand of God brings us closer to him precisely through what happens to us, without us seeking it, and through what affects us negatively.

> The moment has come to plumb the decidedly negative side of our existences—the side on which, however far we search, we cannot discern any happy result or any solid conclusion to what happens to us. It is easy enough to understand that God can be grasped in and through every life. But can God also be found in and through every death? This is what perplexes us deeply. And yet this is what we must learn to acknowledge as a matter of settled habit and practice, unless we abandon all that is most characteristically Christian; and unless we are prepared to forfeit contact with God in one of the most widespread and at the same time most profoundly passive and receptive experiences of human life.
>
> The forces of *diminishment* are our real passivities. Their number is vast, their forms infinitely varied, their influence constant. In order to clarify our ideas and direct our meditation we will divide them into two groups corresponding to the two forms under which we considered the forces of growth: the diminishments whose origin lies *within us*, and the diminishments whose origin lies *outside us*.
>
> The external passivities of diminishment are all our bits of ill fortune. We have only to look back on our lives to see them springing up on all sides....
>
> Humanly speaking, the internal passivities of diminishment form the darkest element and the most despairingly useless years of our life....
>
> In death, as in an ocean, all our slow or swift diminishments flow out and merge. Death is the sum and consummation of all our diminishments: it is evil

itself—purely physical evil; in so far as it results organically in the manifold structure of that physical nature in which we are immersed—but a moral evil too, in so far as in the society to which we belong, or in ourselves, the wrong use of our freedom, by spreading disorder, converts this manifold complexity of our nature into the source of all evil and all corruption.[16]

THE DIVINIZATION OF PASSIVITIES

Just as Teilhard did with activities, he also believes in the divinization of passivities. Perhaps this will be more difficult for us. After all, they are the negative side of our life, and we have to struggle to integrate them into ourselves. Death is always present on the horizon of passivities. That is why Teilhard begins by telling us that for the Christian death is not the end, since Christ has conquered death—it is the beginning of a new life. In this way, what would be the most radical of the passivities becomes the transition to a new life. Death is thus the condition for the divine fire to descend upon us and for us to begin the true life. All the passivities of life become steps toward that final victory of all passivity, both external and internal. It is easier to pray from our activities than to do so from our passivities, when we feel the presence and action of what diminishes us instead of recognizing God's action in our lives.

Here again, as in the case of the "divinisation" of our human activities, we shall find the Christian faith absolutely explicit in what it claims to be the case, and what it bids us do. Christ has conquered death, not only by suppressing its evil effects, but by reversing its sting. By virtue of Christ's rising again, nothing any longer kills inevitably but everything is capable of becoming the blessed touch of the divine hands, the blessed influence of the will of God upon our lives. However marred by our faults, or however desperate in its circumstances our position may be, we can, by a total reordering, completely correct the world that surrounds us, and resume our lives in a favourable sense. *Diligentibus Deum omnia convertuntur in bonum* [All things work together for good for those who love God; Romans 8:28]. That is the fact which dominates all explanation and all discussion.

In itself, death is an incurable weakness of corporeal beings, complicated, in our world, by the influence of an original fall. It is the sum and type of all the forces that diminish us, and against which we must fight without being able to hope for a personal, direct and immediate victory. Now the great victory of the Creator and Redeemer, in the Christian vision, is to have transformed what is in itself a universal power of diminishment and extinction into an essentially life-giving factor. God must, in some way or other, make room for himself, hollowing us out and emptying us, if he is finally to penetrate into us. And in order to assimilate us in him, he must break the molecules of our being so as to re-cast and re-model us. The function of death is to provide the necessary entrance into our inmost selves. It will make us undergo the required dissociation. It will put us into the state organically needed if the divine fire is to descend upon us. And in that way its fatal power to decompose and dissolve will be harnessed to the most sublime operations of life. What was by nature empty and void, a return to bits and pieces, can, in any human existence, become fullness and unity in God....

After having perceived you as he who is "a greater myself," grant, when my hour comes, that I may recognise you under the species of each alien or hostile force that seems bent upon destroying or uprooting me. When the signs of age begin to mark my body (and still more when they touch my mind), when the ill that is to diminish me or carry me off strikes from without or is born within me; when the painful moment comes in which I suddenly awaken to the fact that I am ill or growing old; and above all at that last moment when I feel I am losing hold of myself and am absolutely passive within the hands of the great unknown forces that have formed me; in all those dark moments, O God, grant that I may understand that it is you (provided only my faith is strong enough) who are painfully parting the fibres of my being in order to penetrate to the very marrow of my substance and bear me away within yourself.[17]

THE MYSTERY OF EVIL

In the *Exercises*, we are offered two meditations on sins and another one on hell, that is, on the mystery of evil and its consequences. This theme is not absent in Teilhard's work. He deals with it in *The Divine Milieu* under the title "The outer darkness and the lost souls." He recognizes that by showing the light of the divine fire we cannot stop seeing the shadow and emptiness of God's absence and the difficulty of our consideration. Sin and evil, as well as eternal damnation and hell, do not cease to exist just because we want to ignore them. Even though it might be hard, we have to bring them to our prayer. We must accept by faith, as he says, that "there is a mysterious *outer darkness*. Apart from the fire that unites in love, there is another fire which corrupts in isolation...apart from the final aggregation of souls, there is a segregation and an abyss over nothingness." Faced with this mystery, which we too often avoid raising today, we can only pray.

In the foregoing pages (solely concerned with rising towards the divine focus and with offering ourselves more completely to its rays) our eyes have been systematically turned towards the light, though we have never ceased to feel the darkness and the void beneath us— the rarefication or absence of God over which our path has been suspended. But this nether darkness, which we sought to flee, could equally well have been a sort of abyss opening on to sheer nothingness. Imperfection, sin, evil, the flesh, appear to us mainly as a retrograde step, a reverse aspect of things that cease to exist the further we sink into God.

Your revelation, O Lord, compels me to believe more. The powers of evil, in the universe, are not only an attraction, a deviation, a minus sign, an annihilating return to plurality. In the course of the spiritual evolution of the world, certain conscious elements in it, certain monads, deliberately detached themselves from the mass that is stimulated by your attraction. Evil has become incarnate in them, has been 'substantialised' in them. And now I am surrounded by dark presences, by evil beings, by malign *things*, intermingled with your luminous presence. That separated whole constitutes a definitive loss, an immortal wastage from the genesis of the world. There is not only *nether* darkness; there is also *outer* darkness. That is what the Gospel tells us.[18]

OUTER DARKNESS, HELL

The last exercise of the first week is a meditation on hell. Saint Ignatius asks us to open our five senses imaginatively to the sorrows endured in hell. Today, we find this meditation difficult. Teilhard does not avoid the subject, although he admits that "we feel lost at the idea of hell." That is why he begs that "this terrible thing may appear to me as a fortifying, even beatifying comple-ment" that would somehow illuminate the mystery of the divine milieu. Faced with the mystery of hell that we find so difficult to accept today, we pray with Teilhard that Christ increase our total trust in him.

> Of the mysteries which we have to believe, O Lord, there is none, without a doubt, which so affronts our human views as that of damnation. And the more human we become, that is to say conscious of the trea-sures hidden in the least of beings and of the value represented by the smallest atom in the final unity, the more lost we feel at the thought of hell. We could per-haps understand falling back into in-existence...but what are we to make of eternal uselessness and eternal suffering?
>
> You have told me, O God, to believe in hell. But you have forbidden me to hold with absolute certainty that any single man has been damned. I shall therefore make no attempt to consider the damned here, nor even to discover—by whatsoever means—whether there are any. I shall accept the existence of hell on your word, as a structural element in the universe, and I shall pray and meditate until that awe-inspiring thing appears to me as a strengthening and even blessed complement to the vision of your omnipresence which you have opened out to me....
>
> The existence of hell, then, does not destroy any-thing and does not spoil anything in the divine milieu whose progress is all around me I have followed with delight. I can even feel, moreover, that it effects some-thing great and new there. It adds an accent, a gravity, a contrast, a depth which would not exist without it.

The peak can only be measured from the abyss which it crowns....

O Jesus, our splendidly beautiful and jealous Master, closing my eyes to what my human weakness cannot as yet understand and therefore cannot bear—that is to say, to the reality of the damned—I desire at least to make the ever present threat of damnation a part of my habitual and practical vision of the world, not in order to fear you, but in order to be more intensely yours.

Just now I besought you, Jesus, to be not only a brother for me, but a God. Now, invested as you are with the redoubtable power of selection which places you at the summit of the world as the principle of universal attraction and universal repulsion, you truly appear to me as the immense and living force which I was seeking everywhere that I might adore it: the fires of hell and the fires of heaven are not two different forces, but contrary manifestations of the same energy.

I pray, O Master, that the flames of hell may not touch me nor any of those whom I love, and even that they may never touch anyone (and I know, my God, that you will forgive this bold prayer); but that, for each and everyone of us, their sombre glow may add, together with all the abysses that they reveal, to the blazing plenitude of the divine milieu.[19]

SECOND WEEK

The second week of the *Spiritual Exercises* is marked by the central meditations of "The Call of the Temporal King," "The Two Standards," "The Three Pairs of Men," and "The Three Manners of Humility." They prepare us for the following meditations on the incarnation, and the birth and life of Christ, until Palm Sunday. This week also includes important discussions on the life of the retreatant, such as the consideration of states and making a good choice. Therefore, this week focuses on the mystery of Jesus Christ, the incarnate Word of God, his relationship with the person (the call), the conditions of that call in each person's life, and the response expected from them (choice). For his part, Teilhard stresses that God has become present and united in Jesus Christ by the incarnation not only with humanity but with the entire material universe. Thus, for him, the meditations of the second week should be seen from his vision of Christ's presence in the world. This presence forms the basis of what he calls the "Divine Milieu," that is, the world in which Christ is present.

OMEGA CHRIST

For Teilhard, the evolutionary vision of the world that science has discovered, must be convergent, that is, driven by the progress of humanity (noosphere), in which it continues its evolution toward its final completion. This process is carried out by the attraction to itself of what he calls the "Omega Point," which is eventually identified with the God of faith. Moreover, his Christian faith helps him recognize that this Omega Point is Christ, by virtue of being the incarnation of God in the world. Thus, if the world finally evolves into its union with Christ, the cosmogenesis of evolution will become Christogenesis. As Teilhard himself states, "If the world is convergent and if Christ occupies its centre, then the Christogenesis of St. Paul and St. John is nothing else and nothing less than the extension, both awaited and unhoped for, of that noogenesis in which cosmogenesis—as regards our experience—culminates. Christ invests himself organically with the very majesty of his creation."[1] Christ is, therefore, the center toward which all creation eventually converges, the Omega, as well as the Alpha, since all things have been created by him and for him (see Col 1:16). The figure of Christ, the eternal king, suggested by Saint Ignatius, following the model of the temporal king consistent with the mindset of his time, is now, for Teilhard, "the Cosmic Christ," center and origin of the universe. The meditation on "The Temporal King" thus acquires new cosmic dimensions, which Teilhard finds reflected in the texts of Saint Paul. Christ, the incarnate divine Word, is in this way the one who informs and attracts, through his "powerful energy," the whole universe to its culmination in himself. The presence of Christ, as the ultimate purpose of the whole universe, shines forth in all things: "The cosmic influence of Christ is 'sanctifying life,' purifying it, bringing it to its end in the individuals who are born and in the still diffuse pressure and confrontation that represents it."[2]

> Christ is identical with Omega. In order to demonstrate the truth of this fundamental proposition, I need only refer to the long series of Johannine—and still more Pauline—texts in which the physical supremacy of

Christ over the universe is so magnificently expressed. I cannot quote them all here, but they come down to these two essential affirmations: *In eo omnia constant* [Everything is consistent in him; Col 1:17], and *Ipse est qui replet omnia* [He is the one who fills everything; Col 2:10, cf. Eph. 4. 9], from which it follows that *Omnia in omnibus Christus* [Christ is everything in all; Col 3:11]—the very definition of omega. [...]

Having noted that the Pauline Christ (the great Christ of the mystics) coincides with the universal term, omega, adumbrated by our philosophy—the grandest and most necessary attribute we can ascribe to him is that of exerting a supreme physical influence on every cosmic reality without exception.

As we have already seen, in the light of pure reason, nothing in the universe is intelligible, living, and consistent except through an element of synthesis, in other words a spirit, or from on high. Within the cosmos all the elements are dependent upon one another ontologically, in the ascending order of their true being (which means of their consciousness); and the entire cosmos, as one complete whole, is held up, "informed," by the powerful energy of a higher, and unique, Monad which gives to everything below itself its definitive intelligibility and its definitive power of action and reaction.

So, it is that energy, *qua sibi omnia possit subjicere* [that enables him to make all things subject to himself; Phil 3:21], which we must unhesitatingly attribute to the Incarnate Word, if we are not to allow a world to assume greater dimensions, to overflow its limits, around the figure of Christ—a world that would be more beautiful, more majestic, more organic, and more worthy of worship than Christ. [...]

The presence of the Incarnate Word penetrates everything, as a universal element. It shines at the common heart of things, as a centre that is infinitely intimate to them and at the same time (since it coincides with universal fulfilment) infinitely distant.[3]

PRAYER TO THE COSMIC CHRIST

Teilhard addresses his prayer to the Cosmic Christ. Christ is the center of the whole universe, the dominating influence that penetrates, sustains, and attracts us, the cosmic being that envelops us and completes us in the perfection of his unity. Teilhard feels attracted to him and loved by him and he finds the soul and the link of all the efforts of all humanity in the soul of Jesus. In the humanity of Christ, we find a synthesis of all humans and their desires and efforts, the breath that unites and harmonizes all the scattered elements. "Through his Incarnation he entered not only into mankind but also into the universe that bears mankind.... Christ has a cosmic Body that extends throughout the whole universe... [...] The Incarnation is a making new, a restoration, of all the universe's forces and powers; Christ is the Instrument, the Centre, the End, of the whole of animate and material creation; through Him, everything is created, sanctified, and vivified."[4]

To this faith, Jesus, I hold, and this I would proclaim from the housetops and in all places where men meet together: that You do more than simply stand apart from things as their Master, you are more than the incommunicable splendour of the universe; you are, too, the dominating influence that penetrates us, holds us, and draws us, through the inmost core of our most imperative and most deep-rooted desires; you are the cosmic Being who envelops us and fulfils us in the perfection of his Unity. It is, in all truth, in this way, and for this that I love you above all things.

Caught in the flames of a seemingly self-contradictory desire, I thirsted, Lord, *to become more my own self by emerging from myself*; and it is you who, faithful to your promise, quench my thirst with the living Water of your precious Essence, in which he who loses himself finds his soul and the soul of all other men made one with his own.

Already, when I contemplated your Godhead, I had the rapture of finding a personal and loving Infinite; and the association of those words held such sweetness for me that to repeat them seemed a bliss to which there would be no end; it was like the single note produced by the Angel's viol, of which St. Francis never wearied. And now I know more: the very multitude of my race comes to life in your humanity; the breath that gives solidity and harmony to its scattered elements is not a Spirit whose higher nature is disconcerting to us, it is a human soul that feels and vibrates as I do; it is your very soul, Jesus. I know, too, that, in a supreme condescension to my yearning for activity and change, you offer me this higher, definitive, world which you concentrate and shelter in Yourself, but you offer it *unfinished*, so that my life may be enriched by the intense satisfaction of, in some small way, giving You to Yourself. Here, then, is the one thing that matters, absolute and tangible, that I dreamed of assigning as an objective and ideal to all my human efforts: it is the Kingdom of God, whose realization we have to work for, and which we have to win. Your Body, Jesus, is not only the Centre of all final repose; it is also the bond that holds together all fruitful effort. In you, side by side with *Him who is*, I can passionately love *Him who is becoming*. What more do I need for final peace to spread through my soul, in a way for which I could never have hoped, satisfying even its most apparently impossible aspirations for cosmic life?[5]

THE CALL OF CHRIST

The second week begins with the meditation on "The Call of the Temporal King" as an image of the call of Christ, an eternal king, and the person's response to him. Just as Teilhard's vision of the Cosmic Christ has special characteristics, so does his call and our response to it. In this call, Teilhard features the collaboration of humanity in the work for the progress of the world toward its final convergence in Christ himself, stimulated by the power of love. As Teilhard specifies it, it is now the matter of "a new Charity in which all the Earth's dynamic passions combine as they are divinized." Following Christ includes, therefore, all human effort by which we participate and collaborate in the creative work of God. The universe, in this way, does not remain outside the call that Christ makes to us so that we collaborate in his action of bringing the world to its final culmination in him, but is also part of that final incorporation into Christ. From this perspective, the call and our response to it take on new characteristics. As Teilhard says, the traditional "God of the Above" is also the "God of the Ahead," toward whom all creation and, in particular, all human effort tends.

> The time had now come when I could see one thing: that, from the depths of the cosmic future as well as from the heights of Heaven, it was still God, *it was always the same God*, who was calling me. It was a *God of the Ahead* who had suddenly appeared athwart *the traditional God of the Above*, so that henceforth we can no

longer *worship fully* unless we superimpose those two images so that they form *one*.

A new Faith in which the ascensional Faith that rises up towards a Transcendent, and the propulsive Faith that drives towards an Immanent, form a single compound—a new Charity in which all the Earth's dynamic passions combine as they are divinized: I now see with a vision that will never leave me, that the World is desperately in need of at this very moment, if it is not to collapse.

Classical metaphysics had accustomed us to seeing in the World—which it regarded as an object of 'Creation'—a sort of extrinsic product which had issued from God's supreme *efficient power* as the fruit of his overflowing benevolence. I find myself now irresistibly led—and this precisely because it enables me both to act and to love in the fullest degree—to a view that harmonizes with the spirit of St. Paul: I see in the World a mysterious product of completion and fulfilment for the Absolute Being himself....

In a system of Creative Union, it is not only the Universe but God himself who is necessarily "Christified" in Omega, at the upper limits of Cosmogenesis. In other words, "evolved" Monotheism, around which all that is best in the Earth's religious energies undoubtedly seems to be concentrating, is moving to its logical and biological fulfilment in the direction of some Pan-Christism.[6]

THE DIVINE MILIEU

Contemplating the entire universe, including all of humanity and its work, Teilhard discovers that "all around us, to right and left, in front and behind, above and below, we have only had to go a little beyond the frontier of sensible appearances in order to see the divine welling up and showing through."[7] To express this presence of God in the world that makes it the Divine Milieu, Teilhard uses two terms: *transparency* and *diaphany*. They show how God reveals himself to us in the created world. In this way, the divine milieu is manifested to us as "an incandescence of the inward layers of being....The diaphany [whose joys] no power in the world can prevent us from savouring...." The divine surrounds us, penetrates us and shapes us, so that we can say that we actually live immersed in the divine. To recognize the world as the divine milieu is to live truly in the presence of God continuously. To access it is to find the Only Necessary One, the fire that burns our heart, the one that calms, overshadowing other fires which break us up, and the one that comforts us for our false losses. Those who are abandoned to it feel their inward powers clearly directed and vastly expanded, which enables them to avoid the reefs we come across in life.

> The essential marvel of the divine milieu is the ease with which it assembles and harmonises within itself qualities which appear to us to be contradictory.
>
> As vast as the world and much more formidable than the most immense energies of the universe, it nevertheless possesses in a supreme degree that precise concentrated particularity which makes up so much of the warm charm of human persons.
>
> Vast and innumerable as the dazzling surge of creatures that are sustained and sur-animated by its ocean, it nevertheless retains the concrete transcendence that allows it to bring back the elements of the world, without the least confusion, within its triumphant and personal unity....
>
> However vast the divine milieu may be, it is in reality a centre. It therefore has the properties of a

centre, and above all the absolute and final power to unite (and consequently to complete) all beings within its breast. In the divine milieu all the elements of the universe touch each other by that which is most inward and ultimate in them. There they concentrate, little by little, all that is purest and most attractive in them without loss and without danger of subsequent corruption. There they shed, in their meeting, the mutual external-ity and the incoherences which form the basic pain of human relationships. Let those seek refuge there who are saddened by the separations, the meannesses and the wastefulnesses of the world....

By a complementary marvel, the man who aban-dons himself to the divine milieu feels his inward pow-ers clearly directed and vastly expanded by it with a sureness which enables him to avoid, like child's play, the reefs on which mystical ardour has so often foun-dered.[8]

THE DIVINE MILIEU REVEALED BY THE INCARNATION

After meditation on the Kingdom and consideration of the call, Saint Ignatius contemplates the incarnation, asking for "inte-rior knowledge of the Lord, Who for me has become man, that I may more love and follow Him."[9] For Teilhard, the divine milieu has its ultimate foundation in the fact of incarnation. Without the incarnation, the divine milieu would remain in a dream, a mere mysticism or an unsubstantiated desire. It is precisely Jesus of Nazareth, in whom we finally touch the "active centre, the living bond, the organizing soul of the Pleroma" present in the world. In this way, the divine milieu becomes concrete and tangible, mani-fested, as Saint John says, in "what we have seen with our eyes, what we have looked at and touched with our hands, concerning the word of life" (1 John 1:1). Thus, Teilhard can assert that "we shall then see with a wave of joy that the divine omnipresence translates itself within our universe *by the network of the organising forces of the total Christ.*"[10] It is, therefore, the incarnation that the divine immensity uses to divinize the world, transforming it into a divine milieu and how everything in the world becomes incorporated into Christ.

> The immense enchantment of the divine milieu owes all its value in the long run to the human-divine contact which was revealed at the Epiphany of Jesus. If you suppress the historical reality of Christ, the divine omnipresence which intoxicates us becomes, like all the other dreams of metaphysics, uncertain, vague, conventional—lacking the decisive experimental verification by which to impose itself on our minds, and without the moral authority to assimilate our lives into it. Thenceforward, however dazzling the expansions which we shall try in a moment to discern in the resurrected Christ, their beauty and their stuff of reality will always remain inseparable from the tangible and verifiable truth of the Gospel event. The mystical Christ, the universal Christ of St. Paul, has neither meaning nor value in our eyes except as an expansion of the Christ who was born of Mary and who died on the cross. The former essentially draws his fundamental quality of undeniability and concreteness from the latter. However far we may be drawn into the divine spaces opened up to us by Christian mysticism, we never depart from the Jesus of the Gospels. On the contrary, we feel a growing need to enfold ourselves ever more firmly within his human truth. We are not, therefore, mod-

ernist in the condemned sense of the word. Nor shall we end up among the visionaries and the "illuminati."

The real error of the visionaries is to confuse the different planes of the world, and consequently to mix up their activities. In the view of the visionary, the divine presence illuminates not only the heart of things, but tends to invade their surface and hence to do away with their exacting but salutary reality....As we have already abundantly shown, the effect produced upon human activity by the true transformation of the world, in Jesus Christ, is utterly different. At the heart of the divine milieu, as the Church reveals it, things are transfigured, but from within. They bathe inwardly in light, but, in this incandescence, they retain—this is not strong enough, they exalt—all that is most specific in their attributes....

Disperse, O Jesus, the clouds with your lightning! Show yourself to us as the Mighty, the Radiant, the Risen! Come to us once again as the Pantocrator who occupies the old basilicas in the full solitude of their cupolas! Nothing less than this Parousia is needed to counter-balance and dominate in our hearts the glory of the world that is coming into view. And so that we should triumph over the world with you, come to us clothed in the glory of the world.[11]

CHRIST'S PRESENCE IN THE WORLD

Following Teilhard, the contemplation of the incarnation should be considered not only as God becoming man, but as the union in Jesus of the divine Word with the material universe, which opens new visions of his presence in the world. Our vision of God, humanity, and the world changes dramatically with the incarnation. It is the incarnation thus that gives us the full sense of an evolving world. In particular, with the vision of an evolutionary universe, the incarnation itself acquires a new meaning, in which Christ is the ultimate end toward which the whole universe tends and, at the same time, the source of the power that drives it toward that end. Christ is thus the Alpha and Omega of all creation. Teilhard opens our eyes to this new cosmic vision of the incarnation.

> At the same time, too, I see that it is Christ who first makes himself "cosmic" and then in some way makes himself "absolute."…
>
> It is as though we believed in a Christ who diminished the stature of God.…How quickly, however, and how permanently, that fatal suspicion vanishes the very moment we become sensitive to the mysticism of today and so perceive that precisely because of those characteristics that would at first appear to confine him too strictly to the particular, *an historically incarnate God* is on the contrary the only God who can satisfy not only the inflexible laws of a Universe in which nothing is produced or appears except *by way of birth*, but also the irrepressible aspirations of our own mind.
>
> For the basic truth is:
>
> If we say "God of the Above" + "God of the Ahead," what does this new equation, fundamental to all Religion in the future, give us if not an ultimate whose dimensions are "theocosmic," that is christic?
>
> With no limit to his capacity for being extended and adapted to the World's new dimension and, in addition, with an inexhaustible charge of evolutive energy for our hearts—so there is growing in our firmament, to the scale of and at the demand of the Ultra-human, a true *Super-Christ*, in all the radiance of *Super-Charity*.

Because, Lord, by every innate impulse and through all the hazards of my life I have been driven ceaselessly to search for you and to set you in the heart of the universe of matter, I shall have the joy, when death comes, of closing my eyes amidst the splendour of a universal transparency aglow with fire....

It is as if the fact of bringing together and connecting the two poles, tangible and intangible, external and internal, of the world which bears us onwards had caused everything to burst into flames and set everything free....

A fantastic molecular swarm which—either falling like snow from the inmost recesses of the Infinitely Diffuse—or on the other hand surging up like smoke from the explosion of some Infinitely Simple—an awe-inspiring multitude, indeed, which whirls us around in its tornado!...It is in this terrifying granular Energy that you, Lord—so that I may be able the better to touch you, or rather, who knows? to be more closely embraced by you—have clothed yourself for me: nay, it is of this that you have formed your very Body. And for many years I saw in it no more than a wonderful contact with an already completed Perfection....[12]

THE VIRTUES OF THE DIVINE MILIEU: PURITY, FAITH, AND FIDELITY

At the center of the second week, Saint Ignatius places the meditations on "The Two Standards," "The Three Pairs of Men," and "The Three Manners of Humility," which revolve around our willingness and readiness to face Christ's call to follow him. It is a matter of finding out the demands of a specific type of following Christ that he asks us for, and the deceptions into which one can get, as well as the readiness and radicalism in following Christ. A reflection of these attitudes can be found in the three virtues that Teilhard presents in *The Divine Milieu*: purity, faith, and fidelity. As he himself states, "It could be said that three virtues contribute with particular effectiveness towards the limitless concentration of the divine in our lives—purity, faith, and fidelity." In these three virtues, as Teilhard understands them, we can see a reflection of the conditions to follow Ignatian meditations.

> Purity, in the wide sense of the word, is not merely abstaining from wrong (that is only a negative aspect of purity), nor even chastity (which is only a remarkable special instance of it). It is the rectitude and the impulse introduced into our lives by the love of God sought in and above everything.
>
> He is spiritually impure who, lingering in pleasure or shut up in selfishness, introduces, within himself and around himself, a principle of slowing-down and division in the unification of the universe in God.
>
> He is pure, on the other hand, who, in accord with his place in the world, seeks to give Christ's desire to consummate all things precedence over his own immediate and momentary advantage....
>
> Faith, as we understand it here, is not—of course—simply the intellectual adherence to Christian dogma. It is taken in a much richer sense to mean belief in God charged with all the trust in his beneficent strength that the knowledge of the divine Being arouses in us. It means the practical conviction that the universe, between the hands of the Creator, still continues to be the clay in which he shapes innumerable possibilities according to his will. In a word, it is evangelical faith, of which it can be said that no virtue, not even charity, was more strongly urged by the Saviour....

We have only to believe. And the more threatening and irreducible reality appears, the more firmly and desperately must we believe. Then, little by little, we shall see the universal horror unbend, and then smile upon us, and then take us in its more than human arms....

Through fidelity we situate ourselves and maintain ourselves in the hands of God so exactly as to become one with them in their action....

And finally, through fidelity we find ourselves at every moment situated at the exact point at which the whole bundle of inward and outward forces of the world converge providentially upon us, that is to say at the one point where the divine milieu can, at a given moment, be made real for us.

It is fidelity and fidelity alone that enables us to welcome the universal and perpetual overtures of the divine milieu; through fidelity and fidelity alone can we return to God the kiss he is for ever offering us across the world.[13]

THE COMMANDMENT OF LOVE

In the first week, we saw how Teilhard considers love as "the most mysterious of the cosmic energies" present in the universe, and which we find symbolized by the feminine; now we can see it as an explicit commandment of Christ (John 15:12). However, even from this viewpoint of Christian love, for Teilhard, love continues to play an essential role in the evolution of the universe and not only at the level of humanity. "Considered in its full biological reality, love—that is to say, the affinity of being with being—is not peculiar to man. It is a general property of all life and as such it embraces, in its varieties and degrees, all the forms successively adopted by organised matter....Love in all its subtleties is nothing more, and nothing less, than the more or less direct trace marked on the heart of the element by the psychical convergence of the universe upon itself."[14] Considered from this perspective, the mandate of Christian love for neighbor takes on new dimensions, as part of the cosmic energy that drives the universe to its culmination in Christ. However, Teilhard acknowledges the difficulty of the concrete exercise of love to one's neighbor, "the other." In this way, only recognizing Christ in the other enables us to integrate them into our love, as part of the universal movement that brings all humanity to its culmination.

> Christian charity, which is preached so fervently by the Gospels, is nothing else than the more or less conscious cohesion of souls engendered by their communal convergence *in Christo Jesu*. It is impossible to love Christ without loving others (in proportion as these others are moving towards Christ). And it is impossible to love others (in a spirit of broad human communion) without moving nearer to Christ....
>
> The only subject ultimately capable of mystical transfiguration is the whole group of mankind forming a single body and a single soul in charity. And this coalescence of the spiritual units of creation under the attraction of Christ is the supreme victory of faith over the world....
>
> I confess, my God, that I have long been, and even now am, recalcitrant to the love of my neighbour. Just as much as I have derived intense joy in the superhuman delight of dissolving myself and losing myself in the souls for which I was destined by the mysterious affinities of human love, so I have always felt an inborn hostility to, and closed myself to, the common run of those whom you tell me to love....
>
> Grant, God, that the light of your countenance

may shine for me in the life of that "other." The irresistible light of your eyes shining in the depth of things has already guided me towards all the work I must accomplish, and all the difficulties I must pass through. Grant that I may see you, even and above all, in the souls of my brothers, at their most personal, and most true, and most distant.

The gift which you call on me to make to these brothers—the only gift which my heart can make—is not the overwhelming tenderness of those specially privileged affections which you have placed in our lives as the most potent created factor of our inward growth, but something less sweet, but just as real, and more strong. Between myself and men, and with the help of your eucharist, you want the foundational attraction (which is already dimly felt in all love, if it is strong) to be made manifest—that which mystically transforms the myriad of rational creatures into a sort of single monad in you, Jesus Christ. You want me to be drawn towards "the other" not by simple personal sympathy, but by what is much higher: *the united affinities* of *a world for itself, and of that world for God.*

You do not ask for the psychologically impossible—since what I am asked to cherish in the vast and unknown crowd is never anything save one and the same personal being which is yours. Nor do you call for any hypocritical protestations of love for my neighbour, because—since my heart cannot reach your person except at the depths of all that is most individually and concretely personal in every "other"—it is to the "other" *himself, and not to some vague entity around him*, that my charity is addressed.[15]

THE ANNUNCIATION AND MYSTERIES OF MARY

Already in the first week, in the meditation on sins, Saint Ignatius puts "the first colloquy with our Lady, so that the grace of her Son and Lord may fill me." This is how Mary appears for the first time in the text of the *Exercises*. In the second week, she is present more often, in the offering of the meditation on the Kingdom, "before your glorious Mother," and in the meditations on the incarnation, birth, and the hidden life. In the key meditations of the process of the selection of the Two Standards and Three Pairs of Men, the first of the three colloquies is always addressed to Mary. In Teilhard's writings, the Virgin does not appear very often, although she is present. However, in his remarks on the *Exercises*, there are many references to his meditation on Mary and her relationship with the virtue of purity and the feminine in the world. Teilhard uses the term *marial* (Marian) to refer to Mary's presence in the world by sharing in the cosmic character of Christ (Heart of Matter = Heart of Mary = Heart of Christ).[16] Teilhard culminates the presentation of the role of woman and the feminine in the world with the figure of Mary. God's encounter with humanity in Jesus is made true through her. Thus we add, here, a paragraph dedicated to Mary in his poetic work "The Eternal Feminine."

Have we ever thought of the meaning of the mystery of the Annunciation?

When the time had come when God resolved to realise his incarnation before our eyes, he had first of all to raise up in the world a virtue capable of drawing him as far as ourselves. He needed a mother who would engender him in the human sphere. What did he do? He created the Virgin Mary, that is to say he called forth on earth a purity so great that, within this transparency, he would concentrate himself to the point of appearing as a child.

44

There, expressed in its strength and reality, is the power of purity to bring the divine to birth among us. And yet the Church, addressing the Virgin Mother, adds: *Beata quae credidisti* [Blessed is she who believed; Lk 1:45]. For it is in faith that purity finds the fulfilment of its fertility.[17]

Long before man had measured the extent of my power, and divinized the polarity of my attraction, the Lord had conceived me, whole and entire, in his wisdom, and I had won his heart. Without the lure of my purity, think you, would God ever have come down, as flesh, to dwell in his creation? Only love has the power to move being. If God, then, was to be able to emerge from himself, he had first to lay a pathway of desire before his feet, he had to spread before him a sweet perfume of beauty. It was then that he caused me to rise up, a luminous mist hanging over the abyss— between the earth and himself—that, in me, he might dwell among you. Lying between God and the earth, as a zone of mutual attraction, I draw them both together in a passionate union.

Until the meeting takes place in me, in which the generation and plenitude of Christ are consummated throughout the centuries.

I am the Church, the Bride of Christ.

I am Mary the Virgin, mother of all humanity.[18]

THE MYSTERIES OF CHRIST'S LIFE

In the *Exercises* of the second week—from the fifth to the twelfth day—Saint Ignatius proposes the contemplations on the public life of Jesus, from his departure from Nazareth and baptism in the Jordan until Palm Sunday. We have seen how Teilhard had stressed the cosmic aspect of the incarnation, without forgetting that this aspect is based on the concrete life of the historical Jesus. "For (and this may be the most wonderful thing) the Universal Christ, in whom my personal faith is satisfied, is nothing but the authentic expression of the Evangelical Christ."[19] It is important to emphasize that the Cosmic and Universal Christ, highlighted by Teilhard so much, would be totally meaningless without its concrete basis, which is the historical Jesus. Therefore, he raises the question: "What is, when all is said and done, the concrete link which binds all these universal entities together and confers on them a final power of gaining hold of us?"—and answers: "The Word incarnate, our Lord Jesus Christ."[20]

> To this generalization of the Christ-Redeemer into a true "Evolutionary Christ" (He who bears, with sins, the entire burden of the world in progress), to this elevation of the historical Christ to a universal physical function and to this ultimate identification of Cosmogenesis with Christogenesis, it has been possible to object that they run the risk of fading into superhuman or volatilizing in the cosmic, the human reality of Jesus. Nothing seems to me less well-founded than this objection. Rather, the more one reflects on the deep-rooted laws of Evolution, the more one is convinced that the universal Christ could not appear at the end of time on top of the World if he had not previously entered the midst of the way, *by way of birth*, in the form of an *element*. If the Omega Christ is truly the one that keeps the Universe moving, it is precisely its concrete germ, the Man of Nazareth, that makes him bring out (theoretically and historically) all its consistency for our experience. These two terms are intrinsi-

cally mutually binding and cannot be considered in any other way but simultaneously in a truly total Christ....

Creation, Incarnation and Redemption, the three mysteries, seen in this light, do not actually form more in the new Christology than the three facies of the same background process of a fourth mystery (after all, it alone being absolutely justifiable and valid in the views of this thought). It would be appropriate to give it a name on its own in order to distinguish it explicitly from the other three: the Mystery of the Creative Union of the World in God or *Pleromization*.[21]

Teilhard celebrating Mass before the Battle of Douaumont, October 1916.

[A gift from Mémorial de Verdun, Musée de la Bataille. Used with permission.]

Since once again, Lord—though this time not in the forests of the Aisne but in the steppes of Asia—I have neither bread, nor wine, nor altar,

I will raise myself beyond these symbols, up to the pure majesty of the real itself; I, your priest, will make the whole earth my altar and on it will offer you all the labours and sufferings of the world. [...]

My paten and my chalice are the depths of a soul laid widely open to all the forces which in a moment will rise up from every corner of the earth and converge upon the Spirit. ("La Messe sur le Monde," 139)

THIRD WEEK

The third week of the *Spiritual Exercises* is focused on contemplating the passion of the Lord. The contemplation of these mysteries serves to reassure the retreatant in the decision of following Christ, which he has experienced in the second week. The mystery of the cross is, therefore, at the center of the new week. The contemplations range from the Lord's Last Supper to his death on the cross and his burial, forming a single unit. In the preamble to the first contemplation, the key points of the whole week can be already found: the third, to ask for "grief, feeling and confusion because for my sins the Lord is going to the Passion"; the fourth, "to consider that which Christ our Lord is suffering in His Humanity [...] and to force myself to grieve, be sad and weep"; and the fifth, "how the Divinity hides Itself."[1] These are the feelings that Saint Ignatius wants the retreatant to maintain throughout the third week. The selected texts of Teilhard focus on the Eucharist as a sacramental consecration of the world and the sense of the cross that bears all pain of the world.

THE LAST SUPPER AND THE EUCHARIST

The first contemplation involves "how Christ our Lord went from Bethany to Jerusalem to the Last Supper, inclusive."[2] The first preamble takes us to the Last Supper: "After He had eaten the Paschal Lamb and dined, He washed their feet and gave His most Holy Body and precious blood to His Disciples."[3] We begin, in this way, with a contemplation on the mystery of the Eucharist.

As for every Christian, for Teilhard, the Eucharist is in the center of his life and spirituality: "If we look a little more closely, we shall see that we have simply taken another path in order to rejoin the great highway opened up in the Church by the onrush of the cult of the Holy Eucharist."[4] Teilhard emphasizes that it entails an intimate union with the Lord as we receive his body: "The Eucharist is not well explained unless it is based on a way of contact with Jesus that is much more independent of time and the inferior matter of the material conjunction between the Holy Species and us."[5] Moreover, the Eucharist has a universal dimension for him: it is the consecration of the entire universe. "In virtue of this interconnexion, from which nothing is excluded, the whole of nature vibrates to the radiation of the consecrated Host. Every single atom, no matter how humble or imperfect it be, must cooperate, at least through what it repels or reflects, in the fulfilment of Christ."[6] That is why Teilhard can say that all the communions of all humanity and all times form a single communion: "So in the words of the Consecration, *Hoc est Corpus meum*, a mysterious and immense depth of vivification and Incarnation of Divinity can be seen: *God passes through the Cosmos as Bread*, as in a single and Total Host in the process of elaboration, sanctification, creation."[7]

> When the priest says the words *Hoc est Corpus meum* [This is my Body], his words fall directly on to the bread and directly transform it into the individual reality of Christ. But the great sacramental operation does not cease at that local and momentary event. Even children are taught that, throughout the life of each man and the life of the Church and the history of the world, there is only one Mass and one Communion. Christ died once in agony. Peter and Paul receive communion on such and such a day at a particular hour. But these different

acts are only the diversely central points in which the continuity of a unique act is split up and fixed, in space and time, for our experience. In fact, from the beginning of the Messianic preparation, up till the Parousia, passing through the historic manifestation of Jesus and the phases of growth of his Church, a single event has been developing in the world: the Incarnation, realised, in each individual, through the Eucharist.

All the communions of a lifetime are one communion.

All the communions of all men now living are one communion.

All the communions of all men, present, past and future, are one communion.

Have we ever sufficiently considered the physical immensity of man, and his extraordinary relations with the universe, in order to realise in our minds the formidable implications of this elementary truth? [...]

At every moment the eucharistic Christ controls—from the point of view of the organisation of the Pleroma (which is the only true point of view from which the world can be understood)—the whole movement of the universe....

As our humanity assimilates the material world, and as the Host assimilates our humanity, the eucharistic transformation goes beyond and completes the transubstantiation of the bread on the altar. Step by step it irresistibly invades the universe.[8]

THE OFFERING

The celebration of the Eucharist, after the part dedicated to the readings of Scripture, begins with the offering on the altar, in which we offer, starting with ourselves, all the fruits of the earth, symbolized in bread and wine. On the occasions when Teilhard could not celebrate the Eucharist, first at the front and then during his travels, he composed his own *Mass on the World*, in which he offers and consecrates the whole world.[9] It begins with the offering, to which we can join: "I, your priest, will make the whole earth my altar and on it will offer you all the labours and sufferings of the world." The bread and wine of the Eucharistic offering are now the bread of all that is positive in the effort of the work to grow and advance human progress, and the wine represents the negative part of the exhaustion and pain that so often accompany it. The total host that Teilhard presents to the Lord in each new offering is the world itself, in continuous growth and progress through human labor, and the accumulation of sufferings, also present, that needs God's action upon itself for its consecration. An important part of this offering is formed by all humanity, our brothers and sisters. Each and every one of them must be present in our offering, "this restless multitude, confused or orderly, the immensity of which terrifies us." As Teilhard tells us, that forms our bread and our wine, the work and the pain of the world. No element of our life should be left out of our offering that should also extend to the whole universe.

> Since once again, Lord—though this time not in the forests of the Aisne but in the steppes of Asia—I have neither bread, nor wine, nor altar, I will raise myself beyond these symbols, up to the pure majesty of the real itself; I, your priest, will make the whole earth my altar and on it will offer you all the labours and sufferings of the world.
>
> Over there, on the horizon, the sun has just touched with light the outermost fringe of the eastern sky. Once again, beneath this moving sheet of fire, the living surface of the earth wakes and trembles, and

once again begins its fearful travail. I will place on my paten, O God, the harvest to be won by this renewal of labour. Into my chalice I shall pour all the sap which is to be pressed out this day from the earth's fruits.

My paten and my chalice are the depths of a soul laid widely open to all the forces which in a moment will rise up from every corner of the earth and converge upon the Spirit. Grant me the remembrance and the mystic presence of all those whom the light is now awakening to the new day.

One by one, Lord, I see and I love all those whom you have given me to sustain and charm my life. One by one also I number all those who make up that other beloved family which has gradually surrounded me, its unity fashioned out of the most disparate elements, with affinities of the heart, of scientific research and of thought. And again one by one—more vaguely it is true, yet all-inclusively—I call before me the whole vast anonymous army of living humanity; those who surround me and support me though I do not know them; those who come, and those who go; above all, those who in office, laboratory and factory, through their vision of truth or despite their error, truly believe in the progress of earthly reality and who today will take up again their impassioned pursuit of the light.

This restless multitude, confused or orderly, the immensity of which terrifies us; this ocean of humanity whose slow, monotonous wave-flows trouble the hearts even of those whose faith is most firm: it is to this deep that I thus desire all the fibres of my being should respond. All the things in the world to which this day will bring increase; all those that will diminish; all those too that will die: all of them, Lord, I try to gather into my arms, so as to hold them out to you in offering. This is the material of my sacrifice; the only material you desire.

Once upon a time men took into your temple the first fruits of their harvests, the flower of their flocks. But the offering you really want, the offering you mysteriously need every day to appease your hunger, to slake your thirst is nothing less than the growth of the world borne ever onwards in the stream of universal becoming.

Receive, O Lord, this all-embracing host which your whole creation, moved by your magnetism, offers you at this dawn of a new day. This bread, our toil, is of itself, I know, but an immense fragmentation; this wine, our pain, is no more, I know, than a draught that dissolves. Yet in the very depths of this formless mass you have implanted—and this I am sure of, for I sense it—a desire, irresistible, hallowing, which makes us cry out, believer and unbeliever alike: "Lord, make us one."[10]

THE CONSECRATION

Teilhard calls eucharistic consecration "Fire in the World," since it represents the continuation and actualization of the active presence of the incarnation, now in sacramental form. The key phrase is: "Through your own incarnation, my God, all matter is henceforth incarnate," and later he says, "You are incarnate in the World." For Teilhard, the incarnation is not only the presence of God in the man Jesus and through him, participating in all humanity, but the presence of God in the entire material universe through, exactly, his incarnation in the man Jesus. In this way, he distinguishes the presence by creation ("Fire *over* the World") from the presence by incarnation ("Fire *in* the World"). This presence continues and is being actualized in the Eucharist. Thus, Teilhard, speaking to Christ, can exclaim, "That in every creature I may discover and sense you." This vision of the incarnation, spreading across the entire material universe through the Eucharist, reveals to us what he calls the "diaphany" or transparency of God in the world.

A world that becomes open to the presence of God, through Christ.

> Once again the Fire has penetrated the earth. Not with sudden crash of thunderbolt, riving the mountaintops: does the Master break down doors to enter his own home?
>
> Without earthquake, or thunderclap: the flame has lit up the whole world from within. All things individually and collectively are penetrated and flooded by it, from the inmost core of the tiniest atom to the mighty sweep of the most universal laws of being: so naturally has it flooded every element, every energy, every connecting-link in the unity of our cosmos; that one might suppose the cosmos to have burst spontaneously into flame.
>
> In the new humanity which is begotten today the Word prolongs the unending act of his own birth; and by virtue of his immersion in the world's womb the great waters of the kingdom of matter have, without even a ripple, been endued with life. No visible tremor marks this inexpressible transformation; and yet, mysteriously and in very truth, at the touch of the supersubstantial Word the immense host which is the universe is made flesh. Through your own incarnation, my God, all matter is henceforth incarnate....
>
> Grant, Lord, that your descent into the universal Species may not be for me just something loved and cherished, like the fruit of some philosophical speculation, but may become for me truly a real Presence.

Whether we like it or not by power and by right you are incarnate in the world and we are all of us dependent upon you. But in fact you are far, and how far, from being equally close to us all. We are carried, all together, to the bosom of the same World; yet each of us is our own little microcosm in which the Incarnation is wrought independently with degrees of intensity, and shades that are incommunicable. And that is why, in our prayer at the altar, we ask that the consecration may be brought about *for us: Ut nobis Corpus et Sanguis fiat* [Let it become for us the Body and Blood].... If I firmly believe that everything around me is the body and blood of the Word, then for me (and in one sense for me alone) is brought about that marvellous "diaphany" which causes the luminous warmth of a single life to be objectively discernible in and to shine forth from the depths of every event, every element: whereas if, unhappily, my faith should flag, at once the light is quenched and everything becomes darkened, everything disintegrates.[11]

THE COMMUNION

In the celebration of the Eucharist, consecration is followed by communion, our participation in the body and blood of Christ, which are given to us as food and drink. As in the offerings and consecration, communion also spreads across the whole universe, in which Christ is present. The bread and wine of eucharistic consecration, symbols of human effort and suffering, are to be received in communion with the world. Thus, Teilhard says, "I shall stretch out my hand unhesitatingly towards the fiery bread which you set before me" and "pouring into my chalice the bitterness of all separations, of all limitations [...] you then hold it out to me, 'Drink ye all of this.' How could I refuse this chalice [...]?" But communion is not only this participation in the positive and negative of the world, but through them, in whom the Lord is present, it means being possessed by Christ: "Lord Jesus, I am willing to be possessed by you." This is how, through the forces of the earth, we achieve communion with God. Through them, in a mysterious way, in addition to our participation in Christ, the very growth of the Total Christ is also carried out, to which the whole world is being added. "In conclusion, the whole life of the Christian, both on earth and in heaven, is integrated in a kind of a perpetual eucharistic union. The Divine never reaches us but is communicated by Jesus Christ: this is the essential law of our spiritual life."[12]

First of all I shall stretch out my hand unhesitatingly towards the fiery bread which you set before me. This bread, in which you have planted the seed of all that is to develop in the future, I recognize as containing the source and the secret of that destiny you have chosen for me. To take it is, I know, to surrender myself to forces which will tear me away painfully from myself in order to drive me into danger, into laborious undertakings, into a constant renewal of ideas, into an austere detachment where my affections are concerned. To eat it is to acquire a taste and an affinity for that which in everything is above everything—a taste and an affinity which will henceforward make impossible for me all the joys by which my life has been warmed. Lord Jesus, I am willing to be possessed by you, to be bound to your body and led by its inexpressible power towards those solitary heights which by myself I should never dare to climb. Instinctively, like all mankind, I would rather set up my tent here below on some hilltop of my own choosing. I am afraid, too, like all my fellowmen, of the future too heavy with mystery and too wholly new, towards which time is driving me. Then like these men I wonder anxiously where life is leading me....May this communion of bread with the Christ clothed in the powers which dilate the world free me from my timidities and my heedlessness! In the whirlpool of conflicts and energies out of which must develop my power to apprehend and experience your holy presence, I throw myself, my God, on your word. The man who is filled with an impassioned love of Jesus hidden in the forces which bring increase to the earth, him the earth will lift up, like a mother, in the immensity of her arms, and will enable him to contemplate the face of God....

How could I refuse this chalice, Lord, now that through the bread you have given me there has crept into the marrow of my being an inextinguishable longing to be united with you beyond life; through death? The consecration of the world would have remained incomplete, a moment ago, had you not with special love vitalized for those who believe, not only the life-bringing forces, but also those which bring death. My communion would be incomplete—would, quite simply, not be Christian—if, together with the gains which this new day brings me, I did not also accept, in my own name and in the name of the World, as the most immediate sharing in your own being, those processes, hidden or manifest, of enfeeblement, of ageing, of death, which unceasingly consume the universe, to its salvation or its condemnation. My God, I deliver myself up with utter abandon to those fearful forces of dissolution which, I blindly believe, will this day cause my narrow ego to be replaced by your divine presence. The man who is filled with an impassioned love for Jesus hidden in the forces which bring death to the Earth, him the Earth will clasp in the immensity of her arms as her strength fails, and with her he will awaken in the bosom of God.[13]

THE CONSECRATION OF THE UNIVERSE

The consecration of the Eucharist, as has already been said, is not limited to bread and wine on the altar but is spread across the whole universe. Teilhard repeatedly highlights this universal sense of the Eucharist: "Since first, Lord, you said, '*Hoc est corpus meum*' not only the bread of the altar but (to some degree) everything in the universe that nourishes the soul for the life of Spirit and Grace, has become *yours* and has become *divine*—it is divinized, divinizing, and divinizable."[14] From the words of consecration (in Latin), Teilhard says, "*Hoc* means precisely all things in the Cosmos, *insofar as* they all finally converge in Christ. In other words, *Hoc* (the only 'christifiable' substance, the only consecrable bread) is the convergent component of the World (the convergence of the world); *Hic* (the only true sacramental Wine) is the Evil (suffering, sin, death) inevitably *manifested* in Things, by the creative effort of convergence—by the communicating process of Convergence of the World—."[15] Thus Teilhard can assert, "The Host of bread, I mean, is continually being encircled more closely by another, infinitely larger, Host, which is nothing less than the universe itself."[16] This vision helps us to understand the Eucharist as the continuation over time of the consecration of the universe that is a consequence of the incarnation.

> When Christ, carrying farther the process of his Incarnation, comes down into the bread in order to dwell there in its place, his action is not confined to the particle of matter that his Presence is at hand, for a moment, to etherealize.

The transubstantiation is encircled by a halo of divinization—real, even though less intense—that extends to the whole universe.

From the cosmic element into which he has entered, the Word is active to master and assimilate to himself all that still remains.

Take up in your hands, Lord, and bless this universe that is destined to sustain and fulfil the plenitude of your being among us.

Make this universe ready to be united with you: and that this may be so, intensify the magnetism that comes down from your heart to draw to it the dust of which we are made.

When that moment comes, Almighty Father, I shall concentrate in myself all the aspiration that rises up towards you from these lower spheres—I shall feel the full force of the yearning that seeks expression in my words—I shall look beyond the white host, accepting its domination, and with all the strength of my desire and my prayer, with all my power, over every substance and every development, I shall pronounce the words: *Hoc est corpus meum* [This is my Body].

The divine work is accomplished. Once again, through the priest, the formative power of the Word has come down upon the world, to overcome its nothingness, its wickedness, its futility, its disorder....

In virtue of this interconnexion, from which *nothing* is excluded, the whole of nature vibrates to the radiation of the consecrated Host. Every single atom, no matter how humble or imperfect it be, must cooperate, at least through what it repels or reflects, in the fulfilment of Christ. Every particle, every process, must, through some part of itself, appear in the definitive reality of Christ....

The universe assumes the form of Christ—but, O mystery! the man we see is Christ crucified.[17]

THE PRESENCE OF THE CONSECRATED HOST IN THE WORLD

The consecration of the whole world by the Eucharist makes the Host itself extend its presence everywhere, filling everything and bringing life to everything. In poetic language, Teilhard expresses how the Host, present in a monstrance for worship, extends its presence and effect across the whole universe: "1) The Host becomes dazzling (all light, all attraction); 2) Then, the illuminated objects falling into it like drops of fire by fusion, an eternal concentration; 3) Then its light and its incandescence illuminate all things and transform everything into a vast nebula."[18] Let us also learn to see how the consecrated Host becomes present in the entire universe, consecrating everything. The Eucharist is thus the sacramental continuation of the presence of God incarnate in the bosom of the world.

> On another occasion, I had knelt before the Blessed Sacrament exposed in a monstrance when I experienced a very strange impression. [...]
>
> I had then the impression as I gazed at the host that its surface was gradually spreading out like a spot of oil but of course much more swiftly and luminously. At the beginning it seemed to me that I alone had noticed any change, and that it was taking place without awakening any desire or encountering any obstacle.
>
> But little by little, as the white orb grew and grew in space till it seemed to be drawing quite close to me, I heard a subdued sound, an immeasurable murmur, as when the rising tide extends its silver waves over

the world of the algae which tremble and dilate at its approach, or when the burning heather crackles as fire spreads over the heath....

So, through the mysterious expansion of the host the whole world had become incandescent, had itself become like a single giant host. One would have said that, under the influence of this inner light which penetrated it, its fibres were stretched to breaking point and all the energies within them were strained to the utmost. And I was thinking that already in this opening-out of its activity the cosmos had attained its plenitude when I became aware that a much more fundamental process was going on within it....

A transformation was taking place in the domain of love, dilating, purifying and gathering together every power-to-love which the universe contains.

This I could realize the more easily because its influence was operative in me myself as well as in other things: the *white glow was active*; the whiteness was consuming all things from within themselves. It had penetrated, through the channels of matter, into the inmost depths of all hearts and then had dilated them to breaking point, only in order to take back into itself the substance of their affections and passions. And now that it had established its hold on them it was irresistibly pulling back towards its centre all the waves that had spread outwards from it, laden now with the purest honey of all loves.

And in actual fact the immense host, having given life to everything and purified everything, was now slowly contracting; and the treasures it was drawing into itself were joyously pressed close together within its living light.[19]

THE SENSE OF THE CROSS, THE CONDITION OF HUMAN EFFORT

In the third week, Saint Ignatius wants us to focus on contemplating the passion of Christ, and thus, in the preamble for the first contemplation, he encourages us to consider "that which Christ our Lord is suffering in His Humanity, […] how the Divinity hides Itself and how It leaves the most sacred Humanity to suffer so very cruelly." And in the second contemplation, he wants us to ask for the "grief with Christ in grief, anguish with Christ in anguish, tears and interior pain at such great pain which Christ suffered for me."[20] Teilhard, for his part, also wants us to seek today first the "meaning of the Cross" linked to the life of humankind, but always remaining the Cross of Christ. Thus, he clarifies: "The sense of the Cross, no longer the simple Cross / the Cross above all / the Cross of atonement, but the Cross as an expression of the ultra-humanization and super-humanization (supernatural) of the World by the unification of convergence, through pain."[21] In this way, "*The doctrine of the Cross harmonizes remarkably* with this new point of view (of an evolving world). The Cross announces and symbolizes laborious resignation, faithfulness to the Evolutionary Duty. The Cross is the way and condition of Progress. The History of the World consists *of a continuous creation* and features a victory over natural death."[22] Seen in this way, the Cross is the symbol of all work and suffering, necessarily inherent in the path of human progress. Thus, Teilhard can affirm, "The royal road of the Cross is no more nor less than the road of human endeavour supernaturally righted and prolonged."

> The Cross has always been a symbol of conflict, and a principle of selection, among Mankind. The Faith tells us that it is by the willed attraction or repulsion exercised upon souls by the Cross that the sorting of the good seed from the bad, the separation of the chosen

elements from the unusable ones, is accomplished at the heart of Mankind....

In its highest and most general sense, the doctrine of the Cross is that to which all men adhere who believe that the vast movement and agitation of human life opens on to a road which leads somewhere, and that that road *climbs upward*. Life has a term: therefore it imposes a particular direction, orientated, in fact, towards the highest possible spiritualisation by means of the greatest possible effort....

And finally by the crucifixion and death of this adored being, Christianity signifies to our thirst for happiness that the term of creation is not to be sought in the temporal zones of our visible world, but that the effort required of our fidelity must be consummated beyond a total transformation of ourselves and of everything surrounding us....

The royal road of the Cross is no more nor less than the road of human endeavour supernaturally righted and prolonged. Once we have fully grasped the meaning of the Cross, we are no longer in danger of finding life sad and ugly. We shall simply have become more attentive to its barely comprehensible solemnity. To sum up, Jesus on the Cross is both the symbol and the reality of the immense labour of the centuries which has, little by little, raised up the created spirit and brought it back to the depths of the divine *milieu*....

The Cross is therefore not inhuman but superhuman. [...] From the very origins of Mankind as we know it, the Cross was placed on the crest of the road which leads to the highest peaks of creation. But, in the growing light of Revelation, its arms, which at first were bare, show themselves to have put on Christ:

Crux inuncta. At first sight the bleeding body may seem funereal to us. Is it not from the night that it shines forth? But if we go nearer, we shall recognise the flaming Seraph of Alvernus whose passion and compassion are *incendium mentis*. The Christian is not asked to swoon in the shadow, but to climb in the light, of the Cross.[23]

THE CROSS AND THE MYSTERY OF EVIL IN THE WORLD

We cannot contemplate the passion of the Lord without bearing in mind the pain and suffering of the world and the mystery of evil that is hidden behind them. Teilhard stresses this idea. Moreover, he relates the mystery of the Cross to the evolutionary process of the world, in the broadest sense, which includes the way of humanity toward its incorporation into Christ, also participating in his Cross and overcoming all problems and difficulties. Evil is unavoidably present too. The Cross thus becomes the necessary instrument in the fight against evil. Love definitely overcomes hatred and evil right on the Cross. Teilhard expresses it in another way, referring to evolution: "The Cross becomes (unceasingly, as opposed to being a sign of atonement compensating for evil) a specific and complete symbol of Evolution (an 'open and personalized' Evolution)."[24]

I declare it with complete sincerity. It has always been impossible for me to feel compassion in front of a crucifix when the suffering is presented to me as the atonement for a fault that, either because there was no need on the part of man, or because it could have been done otherwise, God could have avoided. What are we going to do with this difficulty?

However, everything changes dramatically from the point of view of an evolutionary world, the world we begin to understand. Seeing it in such a Universe, where the fight against Evil is a condition, *sine qua non*, of existence, the Cross takes on a new depth and beauty—precisely the values that can seduce us more. Undoubtedly, Jesus is always the One who bears the sins of the World; moral evil is mysteriously made up for by suffering. But, more fundamentally, Jesus is the one who structurally overcomes in himself and for all of us the resistances to unification represented by the multiple, the resistances to the spiritual ascension inherent in Matter. He is the one who bears the burden, unavoidable for the construction of every form of creation. He is the symbol and action of progress. The complete and definitive meaning of Redemption, which is not just atonement, is to go through and overcome. Just as the full mystery of Baptism is not that of washing (the Greek Fathers had understood it well), but the immersion in the fire of the purifying struggle "to be." We must see no longer the Shadow, but the heat of the Cross.[25]

THE CROSS AND THE SUFFERING OF THE WORLD

Contemplating the Passion, we cannot forget the presence of suffering in the world, both physical and moral. We are more and more aware of this, particularly of the suffering produced by humankind: oppression, persecution, violence, and wars. Teilhard bears them in mind when he states that on Calvary we find "the centre on which all earthly sufferings converge and in which they are all assuaged," which he starts to call "cosmic suffering." In this way, united with Christ on the cross, our participation in the suffering of the world works "like a sacrament, a mysterious union of a faithful with the suffering Christ." United with the suffering of Christ and of all men like that, we can achieve *"sympathy with all suffering, cosmic compassion."*

> Now, Christ did not wish his distressful figure to be no more than a warning permanently dominating the world. On Calvary He is still, and primarily, *the centre on which all earthly sufferings converge and in* which they are all assuaged. We have very little evidence about the way Our Lord *tests* His mystical Body, in order to take delight in it, but we can get some idea of how he can gather to himself its sufferings; and the only way, even, we can appreciate the immensity of his Agony is to see in it an anguish that reflects every anguish ever experienced, *a 'cosmic' suffering*. During his Passion, Christ felt that he bore upon his soul, alone and battered, the weight of all human sorrows—in a fantastic synthesis no words can express. All these he took to himself, and all these he suffered.
>
> Further, by admitting them into the domain of his consciousness, he transfigured them. Without Christ, suffering and sin would be the earth's "human waste." The waste-products of the world's activities would pile up into a mountain of laborious effort, efforts that failed, efforts that had been "suppressed." Through the virtue of the Cross this great mass of debris has become a store of treasure: man has understood that the *most effective means of progress is to make use of suffering, ghastly and revolting* though it be.
>
> The Christian experiences suffering just as other men do. As others, so must he do his best to lessen and

alleviate it, not only by humble prayer but also through the efforts of an industrious and self-confident Science; but when the time comes when suffering is inevitable, then *he puts it to good use.* There is a wonderful compensation by which physical evil, if humbly accepted, conquers moral evil. In accordance with definable psychological laws, it purifies the soul, spurs it on and detaches it. Finally, acting as a sacrament acts, it effects a mysterious union between the faithful soul and the suffering Christ.

If it is undertaken first in a disposition of pliant surrender, and continued in a spirit of conquest, the pursuit of Christ in the world culminates logically in an impassioned enfolding, heavy with sorrow, in the arms of the Cross. Eagerly and wholeheartedly, the soul has offered and surrendered itself to all the great currents of nature. When it reaches the term of all that it has gone through and when at long last it can see things with a mature eye, it realizes that no work is more effective or brings greater peace than to gather together, in order to soothe it and offer it to God, the suffering of the world; no attitude allows the soul to expand more freely, than to open itself, generously and tenderly—with and in Christ—*to sympathy with all suffering,* to *"cosmic compassion."*[26]

PRAYER BEFORE THE CROSS

Contemplation of the mysteries of the Last Supper and the Passion should lead us in a special way to intimate prayer with the Lord. Following this idea, we can join the prayer that Teilhard puts at the end of the *Mass on the World.* It shows Jesus as the one in whom all that our heart craves can be found. We ask that he may act in us, burn us, purify us, set us on fire, and sublimate us until the complete annihilation of our egos, that he may reveal to us his Heart, symbol of a world inflamed by the love that has led him to the cross.

> Lord Jesus, now that beneath those world-forces you have become truly and physically everything for me, everything about me, everything within me, I shall gather into a single prayer both my delight in what I have and my thirst for what I lack; and following the lead of your great servant I shall repeat those enflamed words in which, I firmly believe, the Christianity of tomorrow will find its increasingly clear portrayal:
>
> "Lord, lock me up in the deepest depths of your heart; and then, holding me there, burn me, purify me, set me on fire, sublimate me, till I become utterly what you would have me be, through the utter annihilation of my ego." […]
>
> "Lord." Yes, at last, through the twofold mystery of this universal consecration and communion I have found one to whom I can wholeheartedly give this name. As long as I could see—or dared to see—in you, Lord Jesus, only the man who lived two thousand years ago, the sublime moral teacher, the Friend, the Brother, my love remained timid and constrained. Friends, brothers, wise men: have we not many of these around us, great souls, chosen souls, and much closer to us? And then can man ever give himself utterly to a nature which is purely human? Always from the very first it was the world, greater than all the elements which make up the world, that I was in love with; and never before was there anyone before whom I could in honesty bow down. And so for a long time, even though I believed, I strayed, not knowing what it was I

loved. But now, Master, today, when through the manifestation of those superhuman powers with which your resurrection endowed you, you shine forth from within all the forces of the earth and so become visible to me, now I recognize you as my Sovereign, and with delight I surrender myself to you.

How strange, my God, are the processes your Spirit initiates! When, two centuries ago, your Church began to feel the particular power of your heart, it might have seemed that what was captivating men's souls was the fact of their finding in you an element even more determinate, more circumscribed, than your humanity as a whole. But now on the contrary a swift reversal is making us aware that your main purpose in this revealing to us of your heart was to enable our love to escape from the constrictions of the too narrow, too precise, too limited image of you which we had fashioned for ourselves. What I discern in your breast is simply a furnace of fire; and the more I fix my gaze on its ardency the more it seems to me that all around it the contours of your body melt away and become enlarged beyond all measure, till the only features I can distinguish in you are those of the face of a world which has burst into flame.[27]

FOURTH WEEK

In his *Spiritual Exercises*, Saint Ignatius devotes very little space to the fourth week, dedicated to the mysteries of the risen Christ, and the first meditation he chooses is on the apparition to Our Lady. In the third prelude, we can recognize the spirit of the week as we ask for "grace to rejoice and be glad intensely at so great glory and joy of Christ our Lord," and in the fourth and fifth point, he asks us to consider "how the Divinity…now appears and shows Itself so marvellously in the most holy Resurrection" and "the office of consoling which Christ our Lord bears."[1] In the part containing a list of the contemplations on the mysteries of the life of Christ, there are thirteen contemplations on the apparitions after the resurrection and one on the ascension. Finally, the "Contemplation to Attain Love" closes the *Exercises* and can be considered as a transition from the environment of the *Exercises* to ordinary life, so that through the meditation, we may "be able in all to love and serve His Divine Majesty."[2]

THE RESURRECTION, A COSMIC EVENT

For Teilhard, the resurrection has above all a cosmic character; that is why he says that, after his resurrection, Christ radiates his transforming action over the whole universe. The most highlighted part is the effect of the resurrection on the world, in which Christ reveals himself as its center, extending his influence to the whole universe. Christ in his resurrection shows us that he is the Omega Point of creation, toward which everything ultimately tends. Therefore, everything in the world heads toward him, as do all our actions and works, whatever they may be. In this way, all work united to the risen Christ contributes to the construction of the world.

> And then Christ rose again. We are often too inclined to regard the Resurrection as an isolated event in time, with an apologetical significance, as some small individual triumph over the tomb won in turn by Christ. It is something quite other and much greater than that. It is a tremendous cosmic event. It marks Christ's effective assumption of his function as the universal centre. Until that time, he was present in all things as a soul that is painfully gathering together its embryonic elements. Now he radiates over the whole universe as a consciousness and activity fully in control of themselves. After being baptised into the world, he has risen up from it. After sinking down to the depths of the earth, he has reached up to the heavens. "*Descendit et ascendit ut impleret omnia*" (Eph. 4. 10). When, presented with a universe whose physical and spiritual immensity are seen to be ever more bewildering, we are terrified by the constantly increasing weight of energy and glory we have to attribute to the son of Mary if we are to be justified in continuing to worship him, it is then that we should turn our thoughts to the Resurrection....
>
> When, however, the Christian discovers the grand truth that Christ is the Omega, there is a wonderful transformation of this sterile and disheartening attitude.

If Christ is Omega, nothing is alien to the physical building up of his universal body. Look no matter where, in the endless series of material or living processes that are constantly at work in the world, at any activity you please: however humble and unobtrusive it be, it still—so long as it is carried out with a view to unification—creates an atom of fuller being, and that atom is immediately assimilated for all time, through all that is best in it, by the total Christ. Every process of material growth in the universe is ultimately directed towards spirit, and every process of spiritual growth towards Christ. From this it follows that whether the work to which I am tied by the circumstances of the present moment be commonplace or sublime, tedious or enthralling, I have the happiness of being able to think that Christ is waiting to receive its fruit.[3]

THE UNIVERSAL CHRIST

Regarding the resurrection, another name that Teilhard uses for whom he has called the Cosmic Christ is the *Universal Christ*, that is, Christ who fills everything and is the center and end of everything. The adjective "*universal*" means that everything is included in Christ, and nothing stays out of him. Christ is thus, in the first place, the center of the entire universe, and nothing stays out of his influence, not only in the moral aspect but also in the physical one. Now, at the time when the sciences are showing to us the vision of an immense universe of energy and matter, of galaxies, stars, and planets, arising through a long evolution of billions of years, we cannot be satisfied with an image of Christ that is not the center of this entire immense and wonderful universe, a true Universal Christ. However, Teilhard recognizes that this is not always the Christ presented to us by theologians. But this is the Christ that contemporary humanity longs for, and thus he represents a modern image of the "eternal king" referred to by Saint Ignatius, who already sensed him when he addressed him in the offering prayer in the meditation on the Kingdom as the "eternal Lord of all things." Teilhard concludes, "In short, the fundamental and liberating attitude of the union with the Universal Christ is an extremely simple act, but at the same time extraordinarily abundant, complex, and delicate. It needs to synthesize all that has been acquired from the ancient mystics into a new Mysticism."[4]

> By the Universal Christ, I mean Christ the organic centre of the entire universe:
>
>> *Organic centre*, that is, the centre on which every even natural development is ultimately physically dependent.
>>
>> *Of the entire universe*, that is, the centre not only of the earth and mankind, but of Sirius and Andromeda, of the angels, of all the realities on which we are physically dependent, whether in a close or a distant relationship (and that, in all probability, means the centre of all participated being).
>>
>> *Of the entire universe*, again, that is, the centre not only of moral and religious effort, but also of all that that effort implies—in other words of all physical and spiritual growth.
>
> This Universal Christ is the Christ presented to us in the Gospels, and more particularly by St. Paul and St. John. It is the Christ by whom the great mystics lived: but nevertheless not the Christ with whom theology has been most concerned....

Today, "popular" human and Christian consciousness has the duty of reminding the masters of Israel that the time will never come when we are entitled to fold our arms and rest content with any doctrine, however convenient it may be. "What we are seeking is something that is One, that is organic, because it is thus that Christ is seen by us in the depths of our hearts." In these latter days, this is what many souls are saying.

Is not this because the time has come for the still dormant stem of the tree to resume its growth? It is, surely, no exaggeration to say that a new cycle is opening for the Church, wonderfully adapted to the present age of mankind: the cycle of Christ worshipped through the universe.[5]

PRAYER TO THE GLORIOUS CHRIST

Together with Teilhard, we can therefore pray to the risen Christ, who reveals himself as the "universal milieu in which and through which all things live and have their being," thus being the Universal Christ. For Teilhard, Easter is a "great feast" and so he asks that "Christ may help us understand and make understandable the great mystery of this 'resurrection,' which for me becomes more and more the 'formal' aspect of universalization."[6] Teilhard wished to die on Easter Day and the Lord finally granted it to him. We ask the glorious Christ together with him to draw us into the secret recesses of his inmost heart and to lock us in it, as the "universal milieu in which and through which all things live and have their being."

Glorious Lord Christ: the divine influence secretly diffused and active in the depths of matter, and the dazzling centre where all the innumerable fibres of the multiple meet; power as implacable as the world and as warm as life; you whose forehead is of the whiteness of snow, whose eyes are of fire, and whose feet are brighter than molten gold; you whose hands imprison the stars; you who are the first and the last, the living and the dead and the risen again; you who gather into your exuberant unity every beauty, every affinity, every energy, every mode of existence; it is you to whom my being cried out with a desire as vast as the universe, "In truth you are my Lord and my God."

"Lord, lock me up within you": yes indeed I believe—and this belief is so strong that it has become one of the supports of my inner life—that an "exterior darkness" which was wholly outside you would be pure nothingness. Nothing, Lord Jesus, can subsist outside of your flesh; so that even those who have been cast out from your love are still, unhappily for them, the beneficiaries of your presence upholding them in existence. All of us, inescapably, exist in you, the universal *milieu* in which and through which all things live and have their being. But precisely because we are not self-contained ready-made entities which can be conceived equally well as being near to you or remote from you; precisely because in us the self-subsistent individual who is united to you grows only in so far as the union itself grows, that union whereby we are given more and more completely to you: I beg you, Lord, in the name of all that is most vital in my being, to hearken to the desire of this thing that I dare to call *my* soul even though I realize more and more every day how much greater it is than myself, and, to slake my thirst for life, draw me—through the successive zones of your deepest substance—into the secret recesses of your inmost heart.[7]

THE MYSTICAL BODY AND THE COSMIC BODY OF CHRIST

In his resurrection, Christ shows us, in addition to his Mystical Body, the Church, of which all the elect are members, also his Cosmic Body, which covers the whole universe in a foretaste of the final Parousia, when Christ will be all in all things (see Col 3:11). Thus, the face of Christ is reflected in all things. Nothing stays out of him. In this way, the Mystical Body and the Cosmic Body form one thing, the total and universal Christ.

All these extensions that draw beings together and unify them constitute the *axis* of all individual and collective life. It is in virtue of that axis that we see that Christ has not only a mystical, but a cosmic body, the most impressive description of whose chief attributes we owe to St. Paul—even if he never uses the actual term. And this Cosmic Body, to be found in all things, and always in process of individualization (spiritualization) is eminently the *mystical Milieu*; whoever can enter into that milieu is conscious of having made his way to the very heart of everything, of having found what is most enduring in it. There, neither rust nor worm can penetrate; it is immune from the distress of misadventure; and there both action and love can make themselves felt by every being with the highest degree of immediacy and effectiveness.

At the term of the creative effort, when the kingdom of God has reached maturity, all the chosen monads and all the elect forces of the universe will be fused into God through Christ. Then, through the *plenitude* of his individual being, of his mystical body and his cosmic body, Christ, *in himself alone*, will be the heavenly Jerusalem, the new World. There, the original

Multitude of bodies and souls—vanquished, but still recognizable and distinct—will be encompassed in a Unity that will make of it one single spiritual thing.

All human endeavour, whether in action, in prayer, in peace, in war, in science, or in charity—all must press on to the building up of this blessed city.[8]

That is why it is impossible for me, Lord—impossible for any man who has acquired even the smallest understanding of you—to look on your face without seeing in it the *radiance* of every reality and every goodness. In the mystery of your mystical body—your cosmic body—you sought to feel the echo of every joy and every fear that moves each single one of all the countless cells that make up mankind. And correspondingly, we cannot contemplate you and adhere to you without your Being, for all its supreme simplicity, transmuting itself as we grasp it into the restructured Multitude of all that you love upon earth: Jesus!…

Every affection, every desire, every possession, every light, every depth, every harmony, and every ardour glitters with equal brilliance, at one and the same time, in the inexpressible *Relationship* that is being set up between me and you: Jesus![9]

THE "AMORIZATION" OF THE UNIVERSE

The final contemplation of the *Exercises* is the "Contemplation to Attain Love." Saint Ignatius begins it by defining love: "Love ought to be put more in deeds than in words [...] Love consists in interchange between the two parties; that is to say in the lover's giving and communicating to the beloved what he has or out of what he has or can."[10] In this contemplation, we ask for "interior knowledge of so great good received, in order that […] I may be able in all to love and serve His Divine Majesty."[11] Teilhard generalizes the sense of love by giving it a cosmic meaning, so, as we have already seen, he says, "Love is the most universal, the most formidable and the most mysterious of cosmic energies." In this way, he concludes: "The most telling and profound way of describing the evolution of the universe would undoubtedly be to trace the evolution of love."[12] Love thus becomes the ultimate goal of evolution, which consists in the ultimate union of the world in Omega Christ.

> During the course of my life there has gradually been aroused in me, until it has become habitual, the capacity to see two fundamental psychic movements or currents in which we all share, without, however, being sufficiently aware of what they mean….
>
> On one side there was a flux, at once physical and psychic, which made the Totality of the Stuff of Things fold in on itself by giving it complexity: carrying this to the point where that Stuff is made to co-reflect itself. And on the other side, under the species of an incarnate divine being, a Presence so intimate that it could not satisfy itself or satisfy me, without being by nature universal.
>
> This was the double perception, intellectual and emotional, of a *Cosmic Convergence* and a *Christic Emergence* which, each in its own way, filled my whole horizon. Although they both made themselves felt in the very core of my being, it is conceivable that these two new tides of consciousness might have had no effect upon one another—for they reached me from different angles.
>
> But it was not so; and it is precisely this contrary experience that I hope to describe in this essay, for the

delight of my life and all that gives it strength will have been my discovery that when these two spiritual ingredients were brought together, they reacted endlessly upon one another in a flash of extraordinary brilliance, releasing by their implosion a light so intense that it transfigured (or even "transubstantiated") for me the very depths of the World.

I saw how the joint coming of age of Revelation and Science had suddenly opened a door for twentieth-century Mankind into a sort of ultra-dimension of Things, in which all differences between Action, Passion [in the sense of being acted upon] and Communion vanish—not by being neutralized but by reaching an explosive climax: and this at the high temperatures of the Centre and on the scale of the Whole. I saw the Universe becoming "amortized" and personalized in the very dynamism of its own evolution.[13]

CHRIST'S PRESENCE IN THE UNIVERSE

In the second point of the "Contemplation to Attain the Love of God," Saint Ignatius asks us to look at "how God dwells in all creatures, in plants and in animals and in humans," and in the third point, "how God is laboring for me in all the creatures on the earth."[14] Therefore, he wants us to become aware of the presence of God in all things surrounding us. Teilhard extends this presence of God to the whole universe, in his modern evolutionary conception, and regards it as a presence of Christ in his "cosmic" nature. This presence reveals to us the "universality of Christ," the presence of the Universal Christ in the world.

Christian tradition is unanimous that there is more in the total Christ than Mankind and God. There is also

He who, in his "theandric" being, gathers up the whole of Creation: *in quo omnia constant* [in whom all things persist].

Hitherto, and despite the dominant position accorded to it by St. Paul in his view of the World, this third aspect or function—we might even say, in a true sense of the words, this third "nature" of Christ (neither human nor divine, but cosmic)—has not noticeably attracted the explicit attention of the faithful or of theologians.

Things have changed today: we now see how the Universe, along all the lines known to us experientially, is beginning to grow to fantastic dimensions, so that the time has come for Christianity to develop a precise consciousness of all the hopes stimulated by the dogma of the Universality of Christ when it is enlarged to this new scale, and of all the difficulties, too, that it raises.

Hopes, of course: because, if the World is becoming so dauntingly vast and powerful, it must follow that Christ is very much greater even than we used to think.

But difficulties, too: because, in a word, how can we conceive that Christ "is immensified" to meet the demands of our new Space-Time, without thereby losing his personality—that side of him that calls for our worship—and without in some way evaporating?

It is precisely here that we suddenly sense the astounding, liberating, harmony between a religion that is Christic, and a convergent Evolution....

Starting from an evolutionary Omega at which we assume Christ to stand, not only does it become possible to conceive Christ as radiating physically over the terrifying totality of things but, what is more, that radiation must inevitably work up to a maximum of penetrative and activating power.[15]

THE MYSTICAL MILIEU

The resurrection of Christ shows us, by its glorious presence, what the incarnation means for the world—that it is a union of all created and divine things in him. The world seen from this perspective as a mysterious unity of God and the world, is what Teilhard calls the "Pleroma" (fullness), characterized by the action of Christ, and which he also calls the "Mystical Milieu," and it represents completion of the creative union. Man is called to "consecrate the world" by faith in this Milieu and complete it with his work, which he calls "communion with the world." Both in action and in acceptance, we work and suffer with Christ.

> Action and acceptance: these two halves of our life—this inhaling and exhaling of our nature—are transfigured and clarified for us in the rays of creative union. Whatever we do, it is to Christ we do it. Whatever is done to us, it is Christ who does it. Christian piety has always drawn strength from these words of universal and constant union; but has it, I wonder, always been able, or been bold enough, to give to that union the forceful realism that, since St. Paul first wrote these words, we have been entitled to expect? [...]
>
> In the eyes of the believer, the universe is seen to be a flesh. This fact brings us back to the considerations with which earlier we ended our reflexions on the universal Christ. What the mystical vision precisely does—and what the mystical act assists—is to disclose the universal and sacramental consecration of the World.
>
> *To consecrate the world by a complete faith* that makes him see in the infinite network of secondary causes the organic influence of Christ; to *enter into communion with the world* through a complete *loyalty*

in grasping every opportunity of growing greater and in accepting every summons to die—it is to this, ultimately, that the interior life may be summed up for the Christian....

Thus will be constituted the organic complex of God and World—the Pleroma—the mysterious reality of which we cannot say that it is more beautiful than God by himself (since God could dispense with the World), but which we cannot, either, consider completely gratuitous, completely subsidiary, without making Creation unintelligible, the Passion of Christ meaningless, and our effort completely valueless.

Et tunc erit finis [And then it will be the end].

Like a vast tide, Being will have engulfed the shifting sands of beings. Within a now tranquil ocean, each drop of which, nevertheless, will be conscious of remaining itself, the astonishing adventure of the world will have ended. The dream of every mystic, the eternal pantheist ideal, will have found their full and legitimate satisfaction. *Erit in omnibus Deus* [God may be all in all, 1 Cor 15:28].[16]

THE CHRISTIC AND THE DIVINE MILIEU

Finally, the presence of Christ in the world through his incarnation leads Teilhard to consider the world itself as a "christified world," using his terminology. Thus, he will say that the presence of the Omega Christ turns the cosmic dimension of the world into a "christic" dimension, so that the cosmic expands and enlarges the christic and the christic "amorizes" the realm of the cosmic, that is, fills it with energy (energy of love), up to "incandescence." Therefore, what Teilhard calls "the Christic" constitutes for him a synthesis between the *cosmic convergence* and the *Christic emergence*. It thus unites the vision from below with that from above, which can be reached by contemplating the evolving world (Cosmic dimension) and what the Christian faith tells us about Christ, present in the world by his incarnation (Christic dimension). This Christic dimension of the world constitutes what we have already seen as the Divine Milieu.

> With the Christified Universe (or, which comes to the same thing, with the universalized Christ) an evolutionary super-milieu appears—which I have called "the Divine Milieu"—and it is now essential that every man should fully understand the specific properties (or "charter") of that milieu, which are themselves linked with the emergence of completely new psychic dimensions.
>
> All that I have just been saying leads up to this, that what basically characterizes the Divine Milieu is that it constitutes a dynamic reality in which all opposition between Universal and Personal is being wiped out, but not by any confusion of the two: the multiple "reflected" elements of the World attaining their fulfilment, each one still within its own infinitesimal *ego*, by integrant accession to the Christic *Ego*, towards which the totality of Participated Being gravitates; and in so doing, the Participated, in consummating itself, consummates that *Ego* too.
>
> By virtue of this total inter-linking of convergence, no elementary *ego* can move closer to the Christic Centre without causing the entire global sphere to be compressed more tightly; similarly, the Christic Centre cannot even begin to communicate itself more fully to the least of the World's elements, without caus-

ing itself to be contained more strictly within the entire integument of concrete realities.

Whether rising or descending, every operation (because of the very curvature of the particular "space" within which it finds completion) is ultimately pan-humanizing and pan-Christifying at the same time.

In this way, for the "informed eye" all opposition disappears between attachment and detachment, action and prayer, investigation and adoration, concentration on oneself and attraction to the Other. And this because God is now available or comprehensible (and even in a true sense attainable) by the enveloping totality of what we call the Evolution in Christ Jesus....

It is here that the power of the "Christic" bursts into view—in the form in which it has emerged from what we have been saying, engendered by the progressive coming together, in our consciousness, of the cosmic demands of an incarnate Word and the spiritual potentialities of a convergent Universe. We have already seen how a strictly governed amalgam is effected, in the Divine Milieu, between the forces of Heaven and the forces of Earth. An exact conjunction is produced between the old God of the Above and the new God of the Ahead.[17]

THE EVER-GREATER CHRIST

At the end of the fourth week, and thus, at the end our *Exercises*, we pray with Teilhard to Christ, present in the universe as its center and appearing to us as "ever greater," without the old cosmos, static and finite, as our background. It is now replaced by the new Cosmogenesis of a dynamic and evolutionary universe, with its enormous dimensions and duration discovered by the sciences.

We can sense in it the mystery of Christ as the final center of convergence of the universe, which we can never fully comprehend: according to Teilhard's expression, the "ever-greater Christ."

> And all this took place because, in a universe which was disclosing itself to me as structurally convergent, you, by right of your resurrection, had assumed the dominating position of the all-inclusive Centre in which everything is gathered together.
>
> A fantastic molecular swarm which—either falling like snow from the inmost recesses of the Infinitely Diffuse or surging up like smoke from the explosion of some Infinitely Simple—an awe-inspiring multitude, indeed, which whirls us around in its tornado!...It is in this terrifying granular Energy that you, Lord—so that I may be able the better to touch you, or rather, who knows? to be more closely embraced by you—have clothed yourself for me: nay, it is of this that you have formed your very Body. And for many years I saw in it no more than a wonderful contact with an already completed Perfection....
>
> Who, then, is this God, no longer the God of the old Cosmos but the God of the new Cosmogenesis—so constituted precisely because the effect of a mystical operation that has been going on for two thousand years has been to disclose in you, beneath the Child of Bethlehem and the Crucified, the moving Principle and the all-embracing Nucleus of the World itself? Who is this God for whom our generation looks so eagerly? Who but you, Jesus, who represent him and bring him to us?
>
> Lord of consistence and union, you whose *distinguishing mark* and *essence* is the power indefinitely to grow greater, without distortion or loss of continuity, to

the measure of the mysterious Matter whose Heart you fill and all whose movements you ultimately control— Lord of my childhood and Lord of my last days—God, complete in relation to yourself and yet, for us, continually being born—God, who, because you offer yourself to our worship as "evolver" and "evolving," are henceforth the only being that can satisfy us—sweep away at last the clouds that still hide you—the clouds of hostile prejudice and those, too, of false creeds.

Let your universal Presence spring forth in a blaze that is at once Diaphany and Fire.

O ever-greater Christ![18]

The Spiritual Exercises with Teilhard de Chardin

Teilhard during an expedition in China (undated).

[A gift from Georgetown University archives. Used with permission.]

Teilhard in India, 1924.

[A gift from Georgetown University archives. Used with permission.]

EPILOGUE

The unique characteristics of Teilhard's spirituality, marked by the scientific vision of an evolving world are also reflected in his conception and practice of the *Spiritual Exercises*. We have seen his consideration that the meditations of the *Exercises* had to adapt to the new visions of the modern world, influenced by the progress of science and technology and all the desires of contemporary humanity. In this way, the essential meditations of the *Exercises* ("Principle and Foundation," "The Kingdom," "The Two Standards," "Contemplation to Attain the Love of God," and so on), conceived from the viewpoint of a static universe, should be adapted to the vision of a dynamic, evolving one, which continues into the future through human effort and work. For Teilhard, the evolutionary vision of the world, which the sciences have revealed to us, has to be convergent, that is, led in the present by the progress of humanity (*Noosfera*), in which it continues its evolution, toward its final culmination. This process is carried out by the attraction to itself of the *Omega Point*, in whom his Christian faith lets him discover Christ and call him *Omega Christ*.

These ideas about the new orientations of the *Exercises* according to Teilhard's own Christian vision, which he himself summarizes as "a religion of a *Christified* evolution or an evolved *Christianity*," are present in the texts taken from Teilhard's works, which have been proposed for meditations throughout the four weeks of the *Exercises*. The texts reveal a new perspective of the traditional meditations of the *Exercises* and the most central aspects of Ignatian spirituality. They are the result of a deep mystical experience of Christ's presence in the world, formulated in a new way.

In the first week, Teilhardian asceticism is focused on double purification through *activities and passivities*. Any activity should be seen as part of the person's work leading to the divinization of the world, which progresses, attracted by Christ, to its completion. Passivities include the negative side of the suffering associated with the activity. In the second week, the call of Christ acquires a new meaning. It happens with the vision of the *Cosmic Christ*, center and origin of the universe, and the collaboration of humanity in the work for the progress of the world toward its final convergence in Christ himself, stimulated by the power of love. The last contemplation of the fourth week, the "Contemplation to Attain the Love of God," which should make us aware of the presence of God in all things, is expanded by Teilhard to the whole universe in his modern evolutionary conception and considered as a presence of Christ in his "cosmic" nature. Thus, if the world finally evolves into its union with Christ, the *Cosmogenesis* of evolution will become *Christogenesis*. Finally, Christ's presence in the world leads us to regard the world itself as a *divine milieu* and a *Christified world*.

In this way, the selected texts reveal a new dimension of the *Spiritual Exercises* that remain faithful to the spirit of Saint Ignatius. Thanks to them, we can approach this new perspective that has so far received little attention from both the authors about the *Exercises* and those regarding Teilhard's spirituality.

The picture of the Sacred Heart that Teilhard carried with him for most of his life.

[A gift from Georgetown University archives. Used with permission.]

Jesus: Heart of the World,
the Essence and the Driving Force of Evolution.
Sacred Heart: the Driving Force of Evolution;
the Heart of Evolution.
Universal Jesus. Heart of the Heart of the World.
Center of the Cosmic Sphere of the Cosmogenesis.
Heart of Jesus, Heart of Evolution:
Unite me to you!

(Text handwritten by Teilhard on the back of the picture.)

NOTES

INTRODUCTION

1. Teilhard de Chardin's biographies include: Claude Cué-not, *Pierre Teilhard de Chardin: Les grandes étapes de son évolu-tion* (Paris: Plon, 1958) [Eng.: *Teilhard de Chardin: a biographical study / by Claude Cuénot* (London: Burns & Oates, 1965)]; Rob-ert Speaight, *Teilhard de Chardin: A Biography* (London: Collins, 1967); Mary Lukas and Ellen Lukas, *Teilhard: A Biography* (Lon-don: Collins, 1977); Ursula King, *Spirit of Fire: The life and vision of Teilhard de Chardin* (Maryknoll, NY: Orbis Books, 1998).

2. Quoted in Speaight, *Teilhard de Chardin*, 99.

3. Teilhard de Chardin, *Oeuvres 12: Écrits du temps de la guerre 1916–1919* [*Writings in Time of War*].

4. The references to Teilhard's works refer mainly to his complete original works in French: Pierre Teilhard de Chardin, *Oeuvres*, 13 vols. (Paris: Seuil, 1955–1976).

5. Pierre Teilhard de Chardin, *Notes de retraites, 1919–1954* (Paris: Seuil, 2003).

6. There is an abundant bibliography on the spirituality of Teilhard; from among it, we highlight the following books: Henri de Lubac, *La pensée religieuse du Père Pierre Teilhard de Chardin* (Paris: Aubier, 1962) [Eng.: *The Religion of Teilhard de Chardin* (New York: Desclee Company, 1967)]; Christopher F. Mooney,

Teilhard de Chardin and the Mystery of Christ (Garden City, NY: Doubleday-Image, 1968); Maria Gracia Martin, *The Spirituality of Teilhard de Chardin* (New York: Newman Press, 1968); Robert L. Faricy, *All Things in Christ: Teilhard de Chardin Spirituality* (London: Collins, 1981); Thomas. M. King, *The Way of the Christian Mystics: Teilhard de Chardin* (Wilmington, DE: Michael Glazier, 1988); Édith de la Héronnière, *Teilhard de Chardin, une mystique de la traversée* (Paris: Albin Michel, 2003); Gustave Martelet, *Teilhard de Chardin, prophète d'un Christ toujours plus grande* (Bruxelles: Lessius, 2005); André Dupleix and Évelyne Maurice, *Christ présent et universel: La vision christologique de Teilhard de Chardin* (Paris: Mame-Desclée, 2008); Ilia Delio, *The Emergent Christ* (Maryknoll, NY: Orbis Books, 2011); Leandro Sequeiros, *En todo amar y servir: La diafanía de lo divino en el corazón del Universo* (Seville: Bubok, 2012); Kathleen Duffy, *Teilhard's Mysticism: Seeing the Inner Face of Evolution* (Maryknoll, NY: Orbis Books, 2014); Ursula King, *Christ in All Things: Exploring Spirituality with Teilhard de Chardin* (Maryknoll, NY: Orbis Books, 2016); Agustín Udías Vallina, *La presencia de Cristo en el mundo: Las oraciones de Pierre Teilhard de Chardin* (Santander: Sal Terrae, 2017) [Eng.: *Christ's Presence in the World. The Prayers of Pierre Teilhard de Chardin*]; Jesús Sánchez Valiente, *La espiritualidad de Teilhard de Chardin desde el dominio del mundo* (Seville: Bubok, 2018).

7. "Recherche, Travail et Adoration," in *Science et Christ* (*Oeuvres 9*), 281–89 [Eng.: "Research, Work and Worship," in *Science and Christ* (London/New York: Collins, 1968), 219].

8. *Notes de retraites*, 324–25.

9. Pierre Leroy, *Lettres familières de Pierre Teilhard de Chardin mon ami, 1948–1955* (Paris: Le Centurion, 1976), 145.

10. Dupleix and Maurice, *Christ présent et universel*, 36–39.

11. *Notes de retraites*, 158.

12. *Notes de retraites*, 160.

13. *Notes de retraites*, 332.

14. Louis M. Savary, *The New Spiritual Exercises: In the Spirit of Pierre Teilhard de Chardin* (Mahwah, NJ: Paulist Press, 2010).

FIRST WEEK

1. Ignatius of Loyola, *Spiritual Exercises*, Èulogos, 2007.

2. Pierre Teilhard de Chardin, *Notes de retraites, 1919–1954* (Paris: Seuil, 2003), 108–9.

3. Pierre Teilhard de Chardin, *Journal, 26 août 1915—4 janvier 1919* (Paris: Fayard, 1975), 99.

4. "Mon universe," in *Science et Christ* (*Oeuvres* 9), 65–114 [Eng.: "My Universe," in *Science and Christ* (London/New York: Collins, 1968), 37–56].

5. *Le Milieu divin* (*Oeuvres* 4), 125, 127 [Eng.: *The Divine Milieu* (New York: Harper & Row, Publishers, 1960), 108–9].

6. "La puissance spirituelle de la Matière," in *Écrits du temps de la guerre* (*Oeuvres* 12), 477–79 [Eng.: "The Spiritual Power of Matter," in *Hymn of the Universe* (New York: Harper & Row, Publishers, 1961), 65–68].

7. *Le phénomène humain* (*Oeuvres* 1), 211, 237, 304–5, 320 [Eng.: *The Phenomenon of Man* (New York: Harper Perennial Modern Thought, 2008), 191, 214, 273–74, 287–88].

8. "L'Esprit de la Terre," in *L'Énergie humaine* (*Oeuvres* 6), 40–41 [Eng.: "The Spirit of the Earth," in *Human Energy* (New York: Harcourt Brace Jovanovich, 1971), 32–33].

9. "L'Éternel féminin," in *Écrits du temps de la guerre* (*Oeuvres* 12), 281, 288, 291 [Eng.: "The Eternal Feminine," in *Writings in Time of War* (New York: Harper and Row, Publishers, 1968), 192, 198–99, 202].

10. *Le phénomène humain* (*Oeuvres* 1), 297, 299, 301, 303 [Eng.: *The Phenomenon of Man*, 260, 267, 269, 271–72].

11. *Spiritual Exercises*, no. 43.

12. *Le Milieu divin* (*Oeuvres* 4), 59–62 [Eng.: *The Divine Milieu*, 68–70].

13. *Le Milieu divin* (*Oeuvres* 4), 51–53, 40. [Eng.: *The Divine Milieu*, 62–64, 55–56].

14. *Le Milieu divin* (*Oeuvres* 4), 56 [Eng.: *The Divine Milieu*, 66].

15. *Le Milieu divin* (*Oeuvres* 4), 65–67, 41 [Eng.: *The Divine Milieu*, 72–73, 56].

16. *Le Milieu divin* (*Oeuvres* 4), 81–84 [Eng.: *The Divine Milieu*, 80–82].

17. *Le Milieu divin* (*Oeuvres* 4), 84–85; 93–94, 95 [Eng.: *The Divine Milieu*, 82–83, 88–90].

18. *Le Milieu divin* (*Oeuvres* 4), 188 [Eng.: *The Divine Milieu*, 147].

19. *Le Milieu divin* (*Oeuvres* 4), 189–92 [Eng.: *The Divine Milieu*, 147–49].

SECOND WEEK

1. *Le phénomène humain* (*Oeuvres* 1), 330–31 [Eng.: *The Phenomenon of Man* (New York: Harper Perennial Modern Thought, 2008), 297].

2. Pierre Teilhard de Chardin, *Journal, 26 août 1915—4 janvier 1919* (Paris: Fayard, 1975), 91.

3. "Mon Universe," in *Science et Christ* (*Oeuvres* 9), 82, 85–86 [Eng.: "My Universe," in *Science and Christ* (London/New York: Collins, 1968), 54–57].

4. "La vie cosmique," in *Écrits du temps de la guerre* (*Oeuvres* 12), 67, 68 [Eng.: "Cosmic Life," in *Writings in Time of War* (New York: Harper and Row, Publishers, 1968), 58].

5. "La vie cosmique," in *Écrits du temps de la guerre* (*Oeuvres* 12), 60–61 [Eng.: "Cosmic Life," in *Writings in Time of War*, 51–52].

6. *Le coeur de la matière* (*Oeuvres* 13), 65, 67 [Eng.: *The Heart of Matter* (New York: Harcourt Brace & Company, 1979), 53–55].

7. *Le Milieu divin* (*Oeuvres* 4), 133 [Eng.: *The Divine Milieu* (New York: Harper & Row, Publishers, 1960), 112].

8. *Le Milieu divin* (*Oeuvres* 4), 134, 137–38 [Eng.: *The Divine Milieu*, 113–16].

9. Ignatius of Loyola, *Spiritual Exercises*, Èulogos, 2007, nos. 101, 104.

10. *Le Milieu divin* (*Oeuvres* 4), 149 [Eng.: *The Divine Milieu*, 122–23].

11. *Le Milieu divin* (*Oeuvres* 4), 140–41, 158 [Eng.: *The Divine Milieu*, 117–18, 128].

12. *Le coeur de la matière* (*Oeuvres* 13), 65–68 [Eng.: *The Heart of Matter*, 54–56].

13. *Le Milieu divin* (*Oeuvres* 4), 165, 168–69, 174 [Eng.: *The Divine Milieu*, 132–35, 137–38].

14. *Le phénomène humain* (*Oeuvres* 1), 293–94. [Eng.: *The Phenomenon of Man*, 264–65].

15. *Le Milieu divin* (*Oeuvres* 4), 183, 184–87 [Eng.: *The Divine Milieu*, 144–46].

16. Pierre Teilhard de Chardin, *Notes de retraites, 1919–1954* (Paris: Seuil, 2003), 306.

17. *Le Milieu divin* (*Oeuvres* 4), 168 [Eng.: *The Divine Milieu*, 134].

18. "L'Éternel féminin," in *Écrits du temps de la guerre* (*Oeuvres* 12), 290 [Eng.: "The Eternal Feminine," in *Writings in Time of War* (New York: Harper and Row, Publishers, 1968), 200–201].

19. "Comment je crois," in *Comment je crois* (*Oeuvres* 10), 149.

20. *Le Milieu divin* (*Oeuvres* 4), 148 [Eng.: *The Divine Milieu*, 121–22].

21. "Christianisme et évolution," in *Comment je crois* (*Oeuvres* 10), 211, 213.

THIRD WEEK

1. Ignatius of Loyola, *Spiritual Exercises*, Èulogos, 2007, nos. 193, 195, 196.

2. *Spiritual Exercises*, no. 289.

3. *Spiritual Exercises*, no. 181.

4. *Le Milieu divin* (*Oeuvres* 4), 150 [Eng.: *The Divine Milieu* (New York: Harper & Row, Publishers, 1960), 123].

5. "Note sur l'union physique entre l'humanité du Christ et les fidèles au cours de la sanctification," in *Comment je crois* (*Oeuvres* 10), 24.

6. "Le prêtre," in *Écrits du temps de la guerre* (*Oeuvres* 12), 317 [Eng.: "The Priest," in *Writings in Time of War* (New York: Harper and Row, Publishers, 1968), 208].

7. Pierre Teilhard de Chardin, *Journal, 26 août 1915—4 janvier 1919* (Paris: Fayard, 1975), 90.

8. *Le Milieu divin* (*Oeuvres* 4), 150–51, 153–54 [Eng.: *The Divine Milieu*, 123–25].

9. "La Messe sur le Monde," in *Le coeur de la matière* (*Oeuvres* 13), 139–56 [Eng.: "The Mass on the World," in The *Heart of Matter* (New York: Harcourt Brace & Company, 1979), 119–121]. Thomas M. King, *Teilhard's Mass: Approaches to "The Mass on the World"* (Mahwah, NJ: Paulist Press, 2005).

10. "La Messe sur le Monde," 139–40 [Eng.: "The Mass on the World," 119–21].

11. "La Messe sur le Monde," 145–46, 148–49 [Eng.: "The Mass on the World," 123–27].

12. "Note sur l'union physique entre l'humanité du Christ et les fidèles au cours de la sanctification," in *Comment je crois* (*Oeuvres* 10), 24.

13. "La Messe sur le Monde," 150, 151–52 [Eng.: "The Mass on the World," 128–30].

14. "Le milieu mystique," in *Écrits du temps de la guerre* (*Oeuvres* 12), 189 [Eng.: "The Mystical Milieu," in *Writings in Time of War*, 146].

15. P. Teilhard de Chardin, *Lettres à Jeanne Mortier* (Paris: Seuil, 1984), 87–88.

16. "Mon univers," in *Science et Christ* (*Oeuvres* 9), 94 [Eng.: "My Universe," in *Science and Christ* (London/New York: Collins, 1968), 65].

17. "Le prêtre," in *Écrits du temps de la guerre* (*Oeuvres* 12), 315–316, 317 [Eng.: "The Priest," in *Writings in Time of War*, 207–8].

18. *Journal*, 125.

19. "Le Christ dans la matière," in *Écrits du temps de la guerre* (*Oeuvres* 12), 118–20 [Eng.: "Christ in the World of Matter," in *Hymn of the Universe*, 42–44].

20. *Spiritual Exercises*, nos. 195, 196, 203.

21. *Lettres à Jeanne Mortier*, 88.

22. *Journal*, 190.

23. *Le Milieu divin* (*Oeuvres* 4) 115, 116, 117, 118–119 [Eng.: *The Divine Milieu*, 101–2, 103–4].

24. *Lettres à Jeanne Mortier*, 109.

25. "Christologie et Évolution," in *Comment je crois* (*Oeuvres* 10), 103–4.

26. "La vie cosmique," in *Écrits du temps de la guerre* (*Oeuvres* 12), 77–78 [Eng.: "Cosmic Life," in *Writings in Time of War*, 67–68].

27. "La Messe sur le Monde," 152–53 [Eng.: "The Mass on the World," 130–31].

FOURTH WEEK

1. Ignatius of Loyola, *Spiritual Exercises*, Èulogos, 2007, nos. 221, 223, 224.

2. *Spiritual Exercises*, no. 233.

3. "Mon univers," in *Science et Christ* (*Oeuvres* 9), 92, 96 [Eng.: "My Universe," in *Science and Christ* (London/New York: Collins, 1968), 63–64].

4. P. Teilhard de Chardin, *Lettres à Jeanne Mortier* (Paris: Seuil, 1984), 19.

5. "Note sur le Christ-Universel," in *Science et Christ* (*Oeuvres* 9), 39, 44 [Eng.: "Note on the Universal Christ," in *Science and Christ*, 14, 19–20].

6. *Lettres á Jeanne Mortier*, 94.

7. "La Messe sur le Monde," 154 [Eng.: "The Mass on the World," 131–32].

8. "L'Union créatrice," in *Écrits du temps de la guerre* (*Oeuvres* 12), 223–24 ["Creative Union," in *Writings in Time of War* (New York: Harper and Row, Publishers, 1968), 175–76].

9. "Le milieu mystique," in *Écrits du temps de la guerre* (*Oeuvres* 12), 189 [Eng.: "The Mystical Milieu," in *Writings in Time of War*, 146–47].

10. *Spiritual Exercises*, nos. 230, 231.

11. *Spiritual Exercises*, no. 233.

12. "L'Esprit de la Terre," in *L'Énergie humaine* (*Oeuvres* 6), 40–41 [Eng.: "The Spirit of the Earth," in *Human Energy* (New York: Harcourt Brace Jovanovich, 1971), 33].

13. "Le Christique," in *Le coeur de la matière* (*Oeuvres* 13), 96–97 [Eng.: "The Christic," in *The Heart of Matter* (New York: Harcourt Brace & Company, 1979), 82–83].

14. *Spiritual Exercises*, nos. 235, 236.

15. "Le Christique," in *Le coeur de la matière* (*Oeuvres* 13), 107–108, 109 [Eng.: "The Christic," in *The Heart of Matter*, 93–94].

16. "Mon univers," in *Science et Christ* (*Oeuvres* 9), 102, 106, 114 [Eng.: "My Universe," in *Science and Christ*, 73–74, 77–78, 85].

17. "Le Christique," in *Le coeur de la matière* (*Oeuvres* 13), 110–11, 113 [Eng.: "The Christic," in *The Heart of Matter*, 95–96, 98–99].

18. "Le coeur de la matière," in *Le coeur de la matière* (*Oeuvres* 13), 68, 70 [Eng.: "The Heart of Matter," in *The Heart of Matter*, 56–58].

BIBLIOGRAPHY

CUÉNOT, Claude. *Pierre Teilhard de Chardin: Les grandes étapes de son évolution.* Paris: Plon, 1958.

De LUBAC, Henri. *La pensée religieuse du Père Pierre Teilhard de Chardin.* Paris: Aubier, 1962 (Eng.: *The Religion of Teilhard de Chardin.* New York: Desclee Company, 1967).

De la HÉRONNIÈRE, Édith. *Teilhard de Chardin, une mystique de la traversée.* Paris: Albin Michel, 2003.

DELIO, Ilia. *The Emergent Christ.* Maryknoll, NY: Orbis Books, 2011.

DUFFY, Kathleen. *Teilhard's Mysticism: Seeing the Inner Face of Evolution.* Maryknoll, NY: Orbis Books, 2014.

DUPLEIX, André, and Évelyne MAURICE. *Christ présent et universel: La vision christologique de Teilhard de Chardin.* Paris: Mame-Desclée, 2008.

FARICY, Robert L. *All Things in Christ: Teilhard de Chardin Spirituality.* London: Collins, 1981.

IGNATIUS OF LOYOLA. *Spiritual Exercises.* Èulogos, 2007.

KING, Thomas. M. *The Way of the Christian Mystics: Teilhard de Chardin.* Wilmington, DE: Michael Glazier, 1988.

———. *Teilhard's Mass: Approaches to "The Mass on the World."* Mahwah, NJ: Paulist Press, 2005.

KING, Ursula. *Spirit of Fire: The Life and Vision of Teilhard de Chardin.* Maryknoll, NY: Orbis Books, 1998.

————. *Christ in All Things: Exploring Spirituality with Teilhard de Chardin*. Maryknoll, NY: Orbis Books, 2016.

LEROY, Pierre. *Lettres familières de Pierre Teilhard de Chardin mon ami, 1948–1955*. Paris: Le Centurion, 1976.

LUKAS, Mary and Ellen. *Teilhard: A Biography*. London: Collins, 1977.

MARTELET, Gustave. *Teilhard de Chardin, prophète d'un Christ toujours plus grande*. Bruxelles: Lessius, 2005.

MARTIN, Maria Gracia. *The Spirituality of Teilhard de Chardin*. New York: Newman Press, 1968.

MOONEY, Christopher F. *Teilhard de Chardin and the Mystery of Christ*. Garden City, NY: Doubleday-Image, 1968.

SÁNCHEZ VALIENTE, Jesús. *La espiritualidad de Teilhard de Chardin desde el dominio del mundo*. Sevilla: Bubok, 2018.

SAVARY, Louis M. *The New Spiritual Exercises: In the Spirit of Pierre Teilhard de Chardin*. Mahwah, NJ: Paulist Press, 2010.

SEQUEIROS, Leandro. *En todo amar y servir: La diafanía de lo divino en el corazón del Universo*. Sevilla: Bubok, 2012.

SPEAIGHT, Robert. *Teilhard de Chardin: A Biography*. London: Collins, 1967.

TEILHARD DE CHARDIN, Pierre. *Oeuvres*, 13 vols. Paris: Éditions du Seuil, 1955–1976.

————. *Journal, August 26, 1915 – January 4, 1919*. Paris: Fayard, 1975.

————. *Lettres à Jeanne Mortier*. Paris: Seuil, 1984.

————. *Notes de retraites, 1919–1954*. Paris: Seuil, 2003.

UDÍAS, Agustín. *La presencia de Cristo en el mundo: Las oraciones de Pierre Teilhard de Chardin*. Santander: Sal Terrae, 2017.

Teilhard de Chardin in 1947.

INDEX OF NAMES

INDEX OF TEXTS OF
TEILHARD DE CHARDIN